If Polly looks down from
all of these
flowers among the trees

Placed here at this painful place, where
people remember
her lovely face

She knows there are many working here
to change the
laws and show we care

We gather together in sorrow and grief
we think of this tragedy in disbelief

Now Polly's an angel and heavenly
in as peaceful a place as she could be

We are the ones who bear the sorrow
and struggle to make a safer tomorrow.

Poem left at Polly's shrine in Cloverdale,
California

POLLY KLAAS:
THE MURDER OF AMERICA'S CHILD

BARRY BORTNICK

PINNACLE BOOKS
KENSINGTON PUBLISHING CORP.

For my parents: Linda and Bernard Bortnick

Acknowledgments

Special thanks go to my associates Nickey Hernandez, Clichy Robinson, Kathryn Van Sant, Mike Bortnick, George Cline and Brett Pauly. I must also thank the writers and library staff at the *Santa Rosa Press Democrat* for their help with this project. Members of the Petaluma Police Department, as well as the Sonoma County Sheriff's Department and the District Attorney's Office and the FBI also should be praised for their cooperation. I thank my co-workers at the *Santa Barbara News-Press* for their encouragement as well as my friends at Industry R&D in Los Angeles.

Prologue

Crime was a stranger to the sleepy town of Petaluma, California. A community of 47,000 just forty miles north and about twenty-five years behind the crowds and confusion of San Francisco, the small town was a place so tranquil, so "American" that Ronald Reagan used its hometown atmosphere as an example of innocence lost in the United States.

The families who lived in Petaluma felt secure about the safety of their children. Parents thought nothing of letting their kids play in the streets to well after dark. Homeowners kept their windows open on warm nights. Most people didn't bother to lock their doors. Nothing much ever happened to make people afraid.

That all changed on October 1, 1993.

One

THE BOGEYMAN

"Don't worry. I'm not going to touch you."

Twelve-year-old Polly Hannah Klaas started off the day like most others. She said good-bye to her mom, Eve Nichol, and went to meet her two best friends, Kate McLean and Gillian Pelham, at Petaluma Junior High. At lunch break, the three girls planned a slumber party at Polly's that night. Polly's little sister, Annie, would sleep with their mom in the next room and the teens would pile their sleeping bags into the other bedroom.

After school, Polly rushed home to clean the house for her guests. Following her mom's orders, vacuuming the small bungalow and straightening up the small room she and Annie shared. A girl full of warmth and generosity, Polly loved the idea of being hostess and eagerly awaited her friends' arrival soon after dinner time.

Kate had a big soccer game that afternoon and came home exhausted and a little sick. Her mom considered putting her to bed, when Polly called to find out what time Kate was coming over. After learning that Mrs. McLean was about to put her friend to bed, Polly put on the charm. Kate chatted on the family's portable phone and paced around the home while Polly convinced her to talk to her mom and find a way to get to the party.

"She [Polly] was trying a little flattery and it was charming and cute," she said.

It took some begging from Kate, but in the end, Kate was on her way to a party she'd never be able to forget.

Gillian, a husky twelve-year-old girl with dark hair, arrived first. Her mother, Diana Pelham, dropped her off at about 7:00 P.M. The girl carried a Monopoly game, a sleeping bag and a flannel nightgown her grandmother had bought over the summer. Red stripes and flowers were woven into the garment. Gillian carried the items in a plastic bag from Lucky's, a local grocery store.

Polly and Gillian had known each other for about a year and had grown close during their hours of school band practice. Both played the clarinet, as did Kate. After chatting, they ventured into the warm night air, walked away from the home to get ice cream from a local market just a block away. They returned a short time later and searched for ways to kill time until Kate arrived.

They discovered a Mickey Mouse hat and

an antler cap and put their imaginations to work. They posed motionless on the front porch like animals frozen in time.

"We saw a cute sight," Diana Pelham recalled as she pulled into Polly's street in the family's Plymouth Voyager minivan at 8:00 P.M. "Polly and Gillian [were] perched on the banisters around steps, looking like stone lions with their hands on their knees. They were posing themselves to greet Kate. It was a cute little pose."

Kate, meanwhile, had opted for a costume of her own. Her mother helped her arrange a vagabond motif by dressing her in a tie-dyed shirt and floppy kung fu pants.

While Diana went inside to say hello to Eve, the three girls chatted and planned their night of fun. Soon they were playing makeup, coating Polly's face in white powder and black lipstick. The spooky image made Polly look like a dead person. The girls washed the makeup off because Polly didn't like the creepy appearance.

The windows were open that night with only a sheer fabric coating the glass and keeping the prying eyes of neighbors and strangers from peeking in. The light was on inside Polly's room as she played with her friends and little sister. From the street they might have looked like shadow puppets performing an ancient Balinese saga as they laughed the night away.

* * *

A man in dark clothes watched the girls at a distance. He had a beard, a thick build and dark hair mixed with traces of gray. He didn't belong on the peaceful streets of Petaluma.

Inside the home, Eve Nichol readied for bed. It was nearly 10:00 P.M. when she pulled Annie away from Polly's side so the older girls could enjoy some privacy. She left the girls in Polly's room, closed the heavy wooden door to her own bedroom and went to sleep with Annie. It could not have been a more typical scene, one reenacted in countless homes across the quiet neighborhoods of America. There appeared no reason to suspect anything could happen to three girls tucked safely inside their own home with an adult asleep just steps away.

Diana Pelham spotted the man that evening as she drove away after dropping off her daughter. She saw an odd-looking fellow walk from nearby Wickersham Park toward a playground at Walnut Park just two blocks away from where Polly lived. She remembered the figure wore dark clothing and had a distant look in his eyes.

"He was carrying a bag and walking very

purposefully," she said. "He was not altering his gaze or his pace or anything."

Fourteen-year-old Thomas George, a neighbor of Polly's, played sports with his friends in his Fourth Street driveway and at Wickersham Park that night. He, too, spotted a stranger carrying a sack. The man wore dark clothing, and a long-sleeve shirt, Thomas said. When the boys walked down Fourth Street at about 9:00 P.M. to fetch a video, they saw the stranger standing in front of Polly's house. He was smoking a cigarette.

The husky visitor was still staring at Polly's bungalow when Thomas returned a few minutes later. From the street, the dark man had a clear view of Polly's bedroom.

Taleah Miller saw the stranger, too. The twelve-year-old had gone to the movies that night to watch *The Good Son,* a new Macaulay Culkin flick. The movie started at 8:30 and ended at about 10:00 P.M. Her godfather picked her up when the film let out. When they returned to her home on Fourth Street, she saw a man standing on a nearby corner.

"There are a lot of bums and stuff that walk down the street," she said. "I noticed him because he was just standing there. He wasn't doing anything." She said her godfather got a bad vibe from the dark figure also and told the girl to stay inside the car until the bum walked by.

"I don't like this guy," he'd told her.

When the stranger passed, Taleah got out of the car and went home. She remembered his dark clothes, his combed gray hair and the bag he carried in his left hand.

"He looked at me and slid a hand by his face and then put it down and walked away," she said. "He was walking toward Polly's house."

In some neighborhoods, the stranger's movements might have raised immediate suspicion and brought a call to the cops, but because Polly's house was sandwiched between two city parks that had been frequented by Petaluma's homeless, it seemed routine. Walnut and Wickersham parks had become havens for poor people and had recently caused some residents some worry. The Petaluma City Council outlawed alcohol at Walnut Park in July 1993 after surrounding shop owners and residents complained that the sight of drunks was bad for business.

"Parents didn't take their kids to Walnut Park before the drinking ban," said one neighbor. "Women did not go because there were hard-core drinkers there."

That ban cleaned up Walnut Park, but shifted the burden to Wickersham, a peaceful-looking patch of green, the size of a city block, lined with rose bushes.

"The neighborhood has been hell for many years," the neighbor said. "We have had a lot of problems with drugs and drinking in the park. Everyone has portrayed the neighborhood as perfect, but it is not. Everyone is in denial."

"That neighborhood is picturesque, but it's not very good," Polly's aunt Elizabeth Klaas, later told *The New Yorker* of the park that sat half a block from Polly Klaas's house.

Fourth Street area residents have since formed a neighborhood watch group and pressured the city to ban booze at Wickersham Park as well. Today, neighbors watch each others' backs. But that wasn't the case in fall of 1993.

Slumber parties and beer bans meant little to the darkly dressed man, who had spent much of his life inside a prison cell. For the moment, the stranger was in between jailhouse stints. He had been paroled ninety days earlier from the California Men's Colony in San Luis Obispo. He lived in a halfway house in San Mateo, a thirty-minute drive south of San Francisco. On occasion he visited relatives who rented a small house on an Indian reservation about seventy miles north of Petaluma near the town of Ukiah in Mendocino County. The man had made a couple of runs to their place that summer. The travel route from San Mateo to Ukiah took him right past Petaluma along Highway 101.

He later told authorities that he came to Petaluma that night looking for his mother who lived somewhere in town. He hoped she might give him some cash. The two were not close. But old and bad times were now forgotten. On October 1, 1993 the dark visitor wanted his mother. He walked near the city's downtown and looked for her address in a phone book. She wasn't listed.

With nothing much else to do, he hung out between Walnut Park and the city's post office. He parked his decrepit 1979 Pinto a few blocks from Polly's place, passed a Foster's Freeze hamburger stand and bought a quart of beer from a 7-Eleven. He walked into Walnut Park and drank, then headed back to the convenience store after draining the container. The man next ran into a transient with a gray beard and glasses who offered to sell him a joint of marijuana.

At first, the thick man declined the offer, but changed his mind and took a hit. He smoked the joint, bought a second quart of beer and settled back in the park to enjoy the high. He later claimed the pot was laced with PCP, a powerful drug that can send users into a crazed and violent state. He drained the rest of his beer, then reportedly blacked out.

* * *

Sean Anthony Bush watched videos with his friend Aaron Thomas in the rental unit Thomas leased in Eve Nichol's back yard. Bush had a clear view of his neighbor's back porch. He recalled seeing a "thick" man walking up the home's back steps at about 10:00 P.M. Bush told police the man crouched down and glanced through the home's back windows. Apparently, the video was more enticing, because Bush looked away from the stranger and didn't glance in that direction again until Petaluma police officers shined flashlights into his home about forty-five minutes later.

Polly Klaas and her two schoolmates continued their play. They were giggling on the floor of her bedroom next to the bunk bed which was buried in stuffed animals. They started playing Perfect Match, a board game about dating. Eve Nichol checked on the girls right before going to bed at about 10:00 P.M. The twelve-year-olds were laughing and carrying on, but settled down after Eve requested silence.

Before going to sleep, Eve made sure the front door was locked. She could not remember checking the back door, but recalled the evening had been warm and some windows had been left open when Eve said her last good night.

Polly, dressed in a bright pink T-shirt, which she kept tied at the midriff, and in a short, white denim sports skirt, decided to move the slumber party from her room into the living room so the girls could spread out their sleeping bags. When she opened her bedroom door, the bogeyman stood waiting.

He was big and he held a kitchen knife. Polly let out a soft gasp. The nightmare on Fourth Street had begun.

"Don't scream or I'll cut your throats," the intruder told his helpless audience.

He placed the knife on the bunk bed, ordered them to the floor and demanded they lay face down so as not to see him. The girls were frozen in disbelief and too afraid to cry out, fearing the armed stranger might attack them or go after Polly's mom and young Annie.

"If we'd yelled, Polly's mom would have heard," Kate told *People* magazine. "And this guy would have killed one of us."

He took from his bag several strands of a silky fabric that had been cut with scissors. Next he cut the cords from Polly's Nintendo game and used them to shore up his work.

"He told us to put our hands behind our backs," Gillian said. "We did and he just tied it."

Polly, the prettiest of the three trapped girls, looked older than her years with her flowing brown hair and miniskirt. She started to cry. Kate got scared. The thick man remained composed. He told the girls everything was fine.

"I'm not going to hurt you," he promised.

The girls did just what he told them. They got down on the floor and held still while he placed hoods— made from a silky fabric— over their heads. Some of the makeup left on Polly's face smudged against the inside of the cloth hood. There were a few complaints about the tightness of the bindings after he secured their little wrists behind their backs.

"Please don't hurt my mom and sister," Polly begged the dark figure who loomed above and moved about them with confidence and apparent ease.

For the moment, Gillian remained fearless. She thought the pre-Halloween scare might be a joke her friend had devised. She got a decent look at the stranger and recalled that his face was "short and roundish, but not fat."

"I thought he didn't look mean or anything," Gillian said later.

After Polly complained that the bindings were too tight the man loosened them. Then he started asking questions. He wanted to know who lived in the home and told one of the girls to get up. Kate thought he was talking to her and she began to rise.

"No, I don't mean you," he said, then pushed her to the ground.

The man seemed convinced no adults were in the home.

"We kept telling him there were but he didn't believe us," Kate said.

"Why are there so many people here?" he asked. "There is not supposed to be so many people here.

"I'm not going to hurt you," he assured them. "I'm just doing this for the money."

He asked for cash and the girls told him there was money in a jewelry box. He never touched it. Instead, he picked up Polly and carried her into the night. Before leaving, he told Kate and Gillian to count to one thousand. He said their friend would be back soon. As he walked out with his catch, Kate heard the stranger tell Polly: "Don't worry, I'm not going to touch you."

Asleep with her youngest daughter Annie, Eve Nichol didn't hear the stranger enter her home. She didn't hear him give the frightening orders to the three young girls. She didn't hear their pleas for mercy as he bound them tightly around their small wrists. After all, Eve and the children were protected, inside her quiet house, out of harm's way. Or so she thought.

Most of Petaluma was also asleep as the unknown stranger climbed into his car and drove away from Fourth Street with the helpless young girl hooded and tied inside.

After about fifteen minutes, Gillian and Kate began questioning what had gone on. They turned back to back and pulled at each other's bindings, but instead of loosening the silky material, they only made them tighter. Finally, Gillian squatted on the floor, swung her bound arms over her feet and escaped the bonds, then she freed Kate.

"Kate was convinced we had to go right to Eve. We started walking toward her room."

They awoke Eve at 10:40 P.M. She didn't know what to make of the frantic looks on the young girls' faces. It seemed that only moments before, she'd asked the rambunctious children to quiet down and go to sleep. Suddenly, she had two panicked youngsters on her hands babbling about a stranger and Polly, about things her still-sleepy mind couldn't grasp.

"What are you talking about?" she demanded.

"It's true," Gillian wailed. "He was here, he took Polly."

Eve took another look at the girls' startled faces and called 911.

"I could see the state of the girls," she recalled. "Trauma was setting in."

Before the law arrived, Gillian ran through the house frantically searching for her lost friend. Kate wept.

Police found Polly's room a mess. Pieces from their Perfect Match game lay scattered, the straps on Polly's purse had been cut, drawers were left open and two pairs of leggings were found on the floor. Gillian's flowered nightgown was missing. The rest of the house was untouched, save for a partial palm print left on the top rail of the girls' bunk bed.

The girls were separated and interviewed, while detectives gathered evidence.

Petaluma Police Capt. Pat Parks, a father of three boys, had just gone to bed inside his home in the rural hamlet of Occidental, some twenty miles away from Polly's Fourth Street residence, when the watch officer called to report the shocking kidnapping.

Parks was told that the crime had all the markings of a parent's greatest fear, a stranger abduction. Warnings were sent out to the California Highway Patrol and the Golden Gate Bridge District authorities in case the kidnapper tried to leave Petaluma with the girl. Officers on scene by Polly's house checked the nearby parks and an industrial section of town several blocks away. By early morning, a ground fog had crept in and blanketed parts of Petaluma. At first, investigators thought the suspect had left on foot, but the mist made it impossible to use a police helicopter to search for Polly, Parks said. A bloodhound was called in to help officers smell out the missing girl and her abductor.

For now, authorities had covered the initial bases. Parks sent word to the officers in the field that they had an open book to do whatever was needed to locate the missing child. Parks's wife, Denice, had overheard his phone conversation with fellow officers and immediately volunteered to help. Similar thoughts were already forming in other parts of Petaluma, as patrol cars swarmed to the Fourth Street bungalow. Neighbors grew nervous as officers unwound a bundle of yellow police tape and encircled Polly's home— alerting all that something bad had just occurred.

By 2:00 A.M. on the morning of October 2, 1993, Parks knew the missing girl's name and a few minor facts of the case. As a seasoned cop who had worked the job since 1969, he knew the kidnapping would trigger a panic and bring an onslaught of media attention by sunrise. He knew every parent would be on alert.

"These things tend to wake you up," Parks said. "My wife started asking questions. She was concerned because it involved a little girl. There was an identification with the situation by everyone. We all feel very secure in our homes. This guy had done the unthinkable. He had come and taken this innocent 12-year-old girl out of her house. Anyone with children identified with the situation."

Two

AMERICA'S CHILD

"I saw her as I see my own girls, very happy . . . having a lot of dreams and ambitions."

Polly Klaas wanted to be famous, but not this way. Her nationwide acting debut did not come on the big screen as she had often hoped it would, but rather on an October 5, 1993 broadcast of the crime-busting television show "America's Most Wanted." The real drama that followed over the next two months would make Polly the star of her own primetime tragedy.

A national audience first saw Polly dancing across their TV screens when "America's Most Wanted" aired a home video taken from one of the school plays in which she performed. "I am Pegasus, the winged horse," Polly told the audience as she ran across a darkened stage, her arms fluttering in the air and the green cape she wore flying behind her. Acting was only one of her many talents.

She had a high, sweet voice and a stunning smile. Her hair was full, wavy and brown. Her shiny cheeks were marked with dimples. Her brown eyes were friendly and soft. She told jokes, and impersonated Elvis Presley. She enjoyed Archie comics, Judy Blume books, Mel Gibson movies, and eating popcorn and hot fudge sundaes. She owned two cats named Milo and Spooky. She was the kind of girl everyone loved, who grows up to be high-school homecoming queen, not only because of her outer beauty, but for what's inside as well.

"She wanted to be special," her aunt Elizabeth Klaas told the media. "She didn't want to be compared to anyone."

Her sad legacy would be unequaled. Though hundreds of children are kidnapped each year, few cases generate the kind of compassion and obsession the nation has had with Polly Klaas. The passion touched all levels of society, from school girls who wrote poems about her to Winona Ryder— perhaps the defining actress of Generation X— the actress received a copy of one of Polly's favorite books, *Little Women* after she took part in the search effort. Ryder later starred in a 1994 film adaptation of the novel, which earned her an Oscar nomination for best actress. She dedicated the movie to Polly's memory.

The petite, black-haired actress who starred in *Heathers,* a dark comedy about a high-school serial killer, before gaining national acclaim in the Academy Award-nominated film

The Age of Innocence, grew up in Petaluma and, like Polly, had attended Petaluma Junior High School where both developed a passion for theater. Polly had adored Ryder's movies and wanted to be just like her. Ryder, like so many others who heard about Polly Klaas in the early part of the kidnap investigation, wanted to help find the missing child.

"I started acting when I was 12, Polly's age," Ryder told *People* magazine. "I got a real sense of déjà vu. Because this happened in the community I was raised in and because of the connection I felt when I watched her on 'America's Most Wanted,' and when I talked to the family, I thought it was something that a person in my position, if I could help, I should."

The actress sent out flyers of the missing girl that included a drawing of her abductor. She, like all the other volunteers, wore lavender ribbons pinned to her shirt or sweater to symbolize the community's hope for the missing girl. Lavender was Polly's favorite color.

"I could not sit back and watch something like this happen," Ryder told "America's Most Wanted." "I am lucky to be in a position to get things out there and financially offer what I can. I obviously want Polly back safe."

Ryder offered a $200,000 reward for Polly's

safe return and participated in the search efforts.

Just one day before the abduction, Polly had learned about Ryder's connection to Petaluma. Polly's history teacher told the twelve-year-old about a girl he once knew who had been so shy she never even raised her hand in class, according to an account in *People* magazine. The timid student was Ryder. Polly had been thrilled to hear that story. She wanted to be just like Ryder. Her greatest dream was to meet her film idol.

"All I can say is I really want to meet her," Ryder had said. "We had a lot in common, she went to my school and she wanted to be an actress. I felt drawn to try and help."

So did everyone else. Polly's case held Northern California spellbound.

Polly was a true innocent. A tiny child, just four-ten and eighty pounds, snatched by a huge, armed man at the moment she was about to bloom. The cruelty of it all struck at everyone's heart. It didn't matter if you lived in Petaluma or Pittsburgh.

"I just heard a little girl had been taken out of her house and that might have been the key," recalled Don Harvey a Sonoma County resident who, like thousands of volunteers, joined the search for Polly early on. "You hear stories about kids being kidnapped, beaten and raped all the time, but this time they went right into the little girl's house and stole her out of there. That infuriated me."

Noelle Oxehandler hit upon a common denominator— the childhood fear of monsters and bogeymen hiding in closets— in a piece written for *The New Yorker*.

"For all of us, as children, the bedroom has a dual life. It is the place where we play with friends among our toys," she wrote. "It is the place where, when the lights are off, we lie in fear and discover that even the most familiar outlines of stuffed bear and ruffled curtain can take on terrible form . . . the safe world of toys and friends that parents try to create and maintain is a precarious one."

Oxehandler would later note that her abduction transformed Polly from a kid playing bedroom games into an icon whose image graced wanted posters. Polly's image hit a chord with everyone. There was something about her that made people do more than just watch the drama on television or read about it in their daily newspapers. Volunteers put Polly's needs above their own families.

"I remember everyone having all this hope and being shocked by what had happened," said Maureen Dixon, a mother of two young girls and a Polly Klaas Center volunteer. "Everyone was so positive. Everyone wanted to help, be it getting a stamp or mailing a letter. We had 4,000 people helping out. There was a lot of energy and hope. Very inspiring. A real feeling of camaraderie. We were all there for the same purpose."

Some said it was Polly's image that attracted rescue volunteers, who were drawn to the search center as if called by a power beyond the stars. Others believed the sheer audacity of the crime— the fact that a stranger invaded a little girl's bedroom with her mother one door away— shook the nation's sense of security. Maybe it was simply because everyone identified with her. Polly was only twelve and girlish in every way. Perhaps, it was the compelling pictures of her put out on "America's Most Wanted" and other news shows as the case moved along. Polly looked grown up in one portrait, her dark hair framed a light face as she gave a half smile to the camera. In other pictures, she looked younger than twelve, glancing impishly upward at the camera, with her arms wrapped around her younger sister, Annie. She reminded some people of their own daughters, sisters, nieces and grandchildren. She reminded teachers of past pupils. She prompted school kids across the country to think about classmates and their own safety.

"I'm sorry that man hurt your daughter," a fifth-grader wrote of the case to a local newspaper. "I took acting classes with Polly. She was a great actress. She always had a smile on her face. I had a lot in common with her. I also have the same birthday, so me and my friends are going to say a prayer."

She was the little daughter single men would never bounce on their knees, the kid sister to families blessed with only one child. She was the classroom beauty every shy student wanted to meet.

"I saw her as I see my own girls, very happy, looking forward to a long life, having a lot of dreams and ambitions," Dixon said. "She wanted to make the world a better place. Kids are so idealistic. She still had that, she came across as having that innocence about her."

Almost every police officer, sheriff's deputy and FBI agent who worked the case connected with the haunting pictures that fluttered across Northern California, taped to every window, nailed to every telephone pole and stuffed in every mail box across the state.

"There is a resemblance between my daughter and Polly Klaas," said Sonoma County Deputy District Attorney Greg Jacobs. "Both have similar builds and complexions. It's easy for me to put my daughter's face on her body. That's the hardest part for me."

"America's Most Wanted" did five shows about Polly in two months. The world's media invaded Petaluma. Reporters swarmed outside Petaluma Junior High School to surprise her fellow students and get new angles on the story. The school's parking lot overflowed with television satellite trucks. Their transmission dishes looked like silver mushrooms sprouting in the school's dirt and concrete lot. At times it got so bad that school officials needed a restraining order to keep the media at a friendly distance. Banners flew over downtown Petaluma urging the kidnapper to bring the girl back. Parents lit candles as a sign of promise and volunteers swarmed into the streets hours after the kidnapping. None gave up. Rather than lose steam as the story dragged on, the volunteers gained momentum under the battle cry of the Polly Klaas Center, which organized search parties and took phone tips on where the missing girl might be.

"[There has been] an outpouring of love and support from the community that no one here has ever seen," Eve Nichol told "America's Most Wanted." "So much positive energy going out toward her. She is such a wonderful beautiful happy child, if we spread enough light out there we will get her back."

They called it "Polly Power" and the "Petaluma Miracle." People everywhere were moved by both Polly's parents, Eve Nichol, her mom, and her father, Marc Klaas. But mostly they were touched by Polly and the terrible wrong done to her. When that man crept into her bedroom, he violated not only the sanctity of the Klaas household, but every tender and sweet notion people hold about little daughters being made of sugar and spice. He had trespassed on forbidden turf. He had violated a sacred trust that says children, especially little girls, are safe.

"I'm still kind of discombobulated and in shock," Ryder told *People* magazine in October 1993. "All the things that are good in my life now I got in Petaluma— when I was Polly's age."

Polly's grandparents, B.J. and Joe Klaas, abandoned plans to live in Europe after learning that their son Marc was due to have his first and only child in 1981. Joe and B.J. Klaas bought a home in Carmel to be close to the new angel in their lives.

"The happiest day of my life was when Polly was born," Marc Klaas told *People* magazine.

Polly changed from a toddler to a kindergarten grad in ponytails, to a smiling magician in a red cape at Halloween when she was eight.

Eve and Marc Klaas divorced when Polly, their only daughter, was two years old. The marriage had failed, but they remained on friendly terms. Marc Klaas would often remark that they had an unsuccessful marriage but a successful divorce. Eve later married a

man named Allan Nichol, who had three
children from a prior marriage—two older
than Polly and one about her age. Their
daughter Annie was born in 1987. By most
accounts, Polly got along well with this
mixed bag of siblings. Allan Nichol, an architect, moved the clan around the Bay Area.
By the age of twelve, Polly had lived in Fairfax, Bodega Bay, Santa Rosa and Sebastopol.

By 1992, Eve had separated from Allan,
moved to Petaluma and taken a job working
for a children's clothing company. Polly was
a model for the company's brochure. The
vagabond life gave way to a more stable one,
allowing Polly to stay in the same school system for more than a year. Eve Nichol's older
daughter had made many friends, impressed
her teachers with her bright smile, quick
mind and musical skills.

Despite the odd mix of stepparents, step-
sisters and half-sisters surrounding Polly,
everyone got along pretty well. The sibling
and multi-parental melting pot led *New Yorker*
writer Jeffrey Toobin to observe that Polly
Klaas was America's child not just because the
nation was so moved by her story, but because
she was a true product of modern marriage
in America. Naturally, there was some friction
within the family variety pack.

"Polly tried to please her mom, but she'd
stand up to Allan," her aunt Elizabeth Klaas
told *The New Yorker.* "When one of the other

kids would do the same, Allan would say, 'You're pulling a Polly.' "

Polly spent most holidays and weekends with her dad, who ran a Hertz rent-a-car office in San Francisco's Fairmont Hotel. Wherever Polly's family moved, Marc Klaas was there. He worked as a teacher's aide in some of Polly's schools.

"She was literally Marc's reason for doing everything," said Joe Klaas. "He adored her. They had an incredible relationship. I never was as close to my kids. We got along, and I was a good father, but Jesus, [with Marc and Polly] it was this buddy-buddy thing. I never saw anything like it."

The father-daughter bond was so tight that when the extended Klaas family gathered and teased each other, as was often the case, Polly stood ready and leaped to her father's defense.

"She was extremely protective of everyone," Joe Klaas said. "She would not hurt anyone's feelings. If anyone made a joke about Marc, she would jump to his defense. She thought he was the handsomest, best looking, lovely person on earth. If you said anything funny about Marc, she'd yell, 'He is not!' She was a fighter," Joe added. "She would not put up with crap from anybody."

Polly attended several elementary schools in different communities before Eve separated from Allan and settled in Petaluma with Polly and Annie.

"Polly was just starting her second year in the same school system and it meant a lot to her," Elizabeth Klaas told *The New Yorker* in March 1994. "She loved it there. Still, she was insecure about a lot of things. She thought her stepsister, Jessica, was so much smarter and prettier than she was, so she decided to do something that no one in the family had done—perform."

But on stage Polly's shyness faded. Her junior high school drama teacher, Kathleen Mirtoni, told the *Santa Rosa Press Democrat* that Polly had charisma and was an actress in her heart.

"While Polly was wonderful, she was also a normal kid," Petaluma Police Sgt. Mike Meese said, who has four kids, including a six-year-old daughter. "I knew the impish side of her. She was just a nice, warm human being. She has been elevated to the point of being a little angel looking over America. I call her America's Child because she was truly any one of our children."

Meese remembers the little-girl quirks she had, just like every other kid on the block.

"She would write in her school book about things like the shining sun, unicorns and what she wanted to be when she grew up. She had spelling errors like my kids do," he said.

"She loved to make people laugh," her aunt Marianna Ford told the *Santa Rosa Press Democrat*. "She loved to dress up like an old lady and hobble around with a cane and whack people on the butt."

She also loved imitating chihuahuas.

"She'd stick out her tongue and move her eyes around," schoolmate Jason Hafer told *People* magazine. "When I first met her, she was shy. All of a sudden she blossomed into this hyper, fun person."

In addition to her comic and acting skills, Polly liked music. She studied the clarinet and was good enough to move into the advanced band at junior high. The school's music director, Preston Bailey, recognized Polly's gift right off. A talented musician who plays everything from bass guitar to the piano, Bailey once performed a clarinet duet with Polly. He felt her magic.

"I have something between 400 and 500 students I see once a week," Bailey said. "I can't even get to know all their names, but I knew who Polly was."

Polly had a special gift. She had only studied the instrument for about six months when junior high school began, but she was skilled enough to move to the head of the class. Bailey was so impressed with Polly's talents, he called Eve to find out more about the skinny girl who sat quietly in his room. He told Eve that Polly was doing extremely well—above and beyond the top average. He learned from Eve that Polly carried the instrument around with her all the time and played it constantly. It was part of her.

Bailey has two young daughters, age ten and six. He kept them informed of the kidnapping crisis and let them help out at The Polly Klaas Center. The Bailey girls offered quiet, but necessary, relief for stressed volunteers. They rarely bothered anyone and carried simple notes in their hands asking: "May I get anything for you."

Amid the center's frantic energy, there was need for disciplined and soothing helpers.

"They took a cue from me," Bailey said. "I tried to be solid and supportive through it all. The kids and their little notes would show up right when volunteers needed them. They would retrieve water or doughnuts or whatever was needed. It brought smiles to people's faces."

That's how Bailey saw Polly. To him she was a steady and pleasing force who came to class ready for action. As he looked over a class full of kids, his eyes fell on Polly. She was very refreshing.

"You always have to scan the room as a teacher and pick out the hot spots when some kids goof off," Bailey said. "But as I scanned the room, Polly was always ready. She knew what she was doing."

Not only was the talented twelve-year-old

ready for class, she was ready for the emotional shifts and swaying of her mother's on-again, off-again relationship with Allan Nichol. Eve Nichol had worked as manager for a children's clothing mail-order company called Biobottoms. Polly had posed for the company's catalog. By the fall of 1993, Eve and Allan were considering getting back together and moving out of state. The whole thing put a lot of pressure on Polly, who often looked after young Annie.

Despite Polly's outward strength, all her life she had been afraid of the dark, and fearful that a strange man might take her away. Her family knew of her fears, which led to nervous discussions.

"She was afraid of the bogeyman," Polly's aunt, Juliete Klaas-Puleo told *People* magazine.

"I had the uncanny feeling, everyone in the family had the feeling, the fear that something (bad) would happen to her," Joe Klaas said. "She was just so stunning, an unusually beautiful kid. It was like we were always afraid something might happen to her."

But she was uneasy when it came to anything with the hint of tension or violence. While watching the film, *The Last of the Mohicans* with her grandfather, Polly ducked her head behind the theater seats whenever fighting broke out on screen. She'd leave the room when a violent show was on television and turn her head away from the street when being driven through San Francisco or Oakland.

"She was afraid to look out the window," Joe Klaas said. "She was afraid there would be violence out there. She was extremely sensitive to violence."

She loved stuffed animals and cats and sports. A poster of onetime San Francisco 49er quarterback Joe Montana hung in her room.

"She was a great comedian and was full of jokes," Joe Klaas said. "She could just see things and laugh like hell at things everyone else was taking seriously. Pretty soon, you'd see it her way and start laughing too. There just wasn't a mean bone in her body."

But she feared the dark. Whenever she spent nights with Joe and B.J., Polly camped in their living room, not an upstairs bedroom. Joe and B.J. would leave the French doors to their bedroom open and make sure a light was left on for their grandchild.

"She didn't want to be alone," Joe Klaas told the *Santa Rosa Press Democrat*. "Being alone was frightening to her."

Three

CLOSE CALL

"There's people up there and they'll call the cops."

Twenty-four miles away from Petaluma, on Pythian Road, a narrow, winding and ditch-filled path that overlooked a Sonoma County vineyard and a juvenile detention center, the stranger's Pinto struggled as it sputtered up the steep grade. He ignored the no-trespassing signs and rolled past an open metal gate on private property, then accidentally rolled the car into a ditch. The car was hopelessly snagged like a fox in the jaws of a steel trap. The man knew it was only a matter of time before the two girls he'd left behind would wriggle free from the Nintendo cords and cloth straps, but he knew he wasn't going anywhere fast.

The big man started to sweat.

For the moment, he was still in command on Pythian Road. To stay there he had to get out of the ditch and he had to deal with the girl he had kidnapped. The man figured it would not be long before someone happened by and discovered his trapped car. After all, there were enough no-trespassing signs on this stretch of Pythian Road to scare off a blind man. Still, it was nearly midnight and the surrounding pine trees lent good cover. The skinny brown-haired girl had to be hidden before anyone came by.

While the man pondered his plight on Pythian Road nineteen-year-old Shannon Lynch made small talk with her friend and employer, Dana Jaffe. The two were inside Jaffe's home which stood about 100 yards from the stranded Pinto at the crest of Pythian Road. The driveway path had been clear when Dana came home at about 11:15 P.M. For the moment, all appeared normal. There was time enough for some little chit-chat with the babysitter before she hopped into her Ford Escort at about 11:40 P.M. and rolled down the hill. The day's staid routine was interrupted when she saw the stranger and his lame Pinto.

The Pinto stood twenty to fifty feet inside a metal gate that marked the beginning of property. He eyed the Escort as it inched toward him.

Shannon was surprised at finding a stranger on the isolated land so late at night. She wasn't about to get too friendly with the dark figure. She stopped her car a short distance away, depressed the clutch with her left foot and kept the vehicle running and in gear.

"I drive with my doors locked," she said later. "I mean it was late and I didn't need this guy getting into my car."

She cracked open her driver's side window an inch or so and questioned the man she saw dressed in blue jeans and a dark sweat shirt. Suddenly, he shoved his fingers through the crack in her window and shot out questions. In a commanding voice, he demanded to know what was up the road.

"I'm stuck. I need some rope," he told her.

Shannon was in no mood for a midnight conversation in the woods with a surly stranger.

"What are you doing here?" Shannon yelled. "There's people up there and they will call the cops."

Not waiting for a reply, she gunned the Escort's engine and tore down Pythian Road toward Highway 12 which connects Santa Rosa to the Napa Valley wine country.

She didn't bother to look in the rear-view mirror to see the stranger's reaction. She was full of purpose and panic and feared the bearded man might make his way to Jaffe's house before she could sound the alarm.

Now it was the man's turn to panic. He had few options. Any hope of escaping with the girl undetected was now lost. The woman in the car was aware of danger. He had no escape. He carried Polly up a steep embankment twenty-five to forty yards from his ditched Pinto and hid her in the darkness. The twelve-year-old didn't make a sound.

Shannon negotiated the narrow one-lane road as best she could given her shaken nerves. It took several minutes for her to find a phone booth outside a deli just off the thoroughfare. She dashed out and shoved some change in the machine, but the thing ate her quarter.

"I called the operator and told her it was an emergency," she said.

Emergency or not, the phone company wasn't working for free and the operator demanded payment before placing the call. Shannon used her parents' calling card number to call Jaffe. Dana had already undressed and readied for bed when the phone rang.

"She said someone was on the property and she thought he was walking toward the house," Jaffe said later. "A lot of things went through my mind. I felt vulnerable. I felt like I wanted to confront whoever was on the property on my own terms."

Dana was used to the seclusion of the Sonoma County hills. She wasn't going to let some stranger get to her and her daughter, Kalila. Dressing quickly, Dana told the child that an ugly and scary dude was coming their way. Kalila, obviously cut from the same cloth as her mother didn't bat an eye, assumed an offensive stance, got dressed and searched for weapons. Armed with a bat and a can of Mace, mother and child moved out of the house and into their maroon Toyota wagon. They drove near the Pinto, but did not see the trespasser.

She slowed almost to a stop, glanced inside the stranded car, saw no one and continued down the hill toward the highway. Dana stopped at a little market and also had the phone booth eat her quarter. She found a good phone at a nearby gas station and called the Sonoma County Sheriff's Department. She alerted deputies to the trespasser. There was no reason for anyone to be up in her neck of the woods so late at night.

Friday nights are busy times for cops in most communities. And so it was for Sonoma County Sheriff's Deputies Michael David Rankin and Thomas Michael Howard. They had fights to break up, drunks to stop and a gang-related shooting to worry about. Investigating some trespasser caught creeping around a hilltop did not seem like a crisis. Jaffe waited at the base of Pythian Road for the cavalry to arrive. It took ten minutes.

She led the way and the deputies followed her station wagon in separate patrol cars.

When the three cars passed the metal gate, they found the man smoking a cigarette and leaning against his car. He told them he had accidentally driven onto her land. He said he got stuck trying to get out of the place. It seemed a bit tenuous, but the hour was late, Jaffe was tired. She could have been a stickler and had the stranger arrested for trespassing, but at the time he seemed little more than a nuisance.

She told the deputies she wanted him gone, not jailed. Then she continued driving up the hill and went home figuring Rankin and Howard could deal with the stranger. Dana recalled the man was not wearing a sweat shirt and stood there in a T-shirt. Bits and pieces of brush clung to his hair and clothing as if he'd been rolling around on the ground. The whole thing looked weird to the deputies, but for the moment there was no evidence of a crime.

Rankin, who had been a sheriff's deputy for five years and had spent time in the Army helping counsel drug and alcohol abusers, had grown up in Sonoma County and knew the Pythian Road area well. He figured the man was up to something, and it was probably bad news. Before stepping out of his patrol car, Rankin slid a police baton into the steel ring that clung to his belt. When he got to the man, the trespasser was already talking things over with Deputy Howard.

"I was wondering when somebody was going to drive up here," he said before the deputies could begin their questioning. "A lady just passed here minutes ago and didn't say anything or stop."

The stranger was edgy. He told the sheriffs he was stuck and insisted they use their patrol cars to push his Pinto out of the ditch. Howard got close enough to smell alcohol on the man's breath. He also noticed that the man's forehead was drenched in sweat.

The stranger dabbed his slick brow with his shirt to soak up the perspiration. He showed his cool and provided an excuse when the lawmen asked what he was doing on an isolated dirt road in the middle of the night. The man claimed he was on his way from the Bay Area to his brother-in-law's home 60 miles north of Santa Rosa in the town of Redwood Valley near Ukiah. He said he had never been in this part of Sonoma County before and wanted to check out the sights. He told the deputies he thought the area was real pretty.

"Well, it's pitch dark and you can't see anything," Howard shot back. "I don't really believe you."

The give and take continued but the stranger wasn't giving up much. He stuck to the sightseeing story. Howard continued questioning him while Rankin patted down the trespasser and searched for weapons. He got tense as Rankin continued his search.

"What the fuck are you doing here?" he demanded.

The deputies told him to relax. When the man finally figured out that all this attention was for simple trespass, he mellowed out while Rankin continued to search for weapons. The only thing Rankin uncovered was a flashlight. Other than that, the scary-looking dude was clean. They put him through the usual roadside tests for drugs and alcohol, took his license and ran the information to see if he was wanted for any current crimes. The cursory check did not include a full background review since that information was not then available for officers in the field. Had Rankin and Howard been back at the station, or had their patrol cars been equipped with a more advanced computer system, they could have run a detailed criminal history. Had that occurred, they would have had a better understanding of Richard Allen Davis. They would have discovered that he was freshly paroled from a state prison in San Luis Obispo after serving eight years for kidnapping and robbery. A trespassing charge could have violated the terms of his parole and sent Davis back to jail. A detailed background check would have turned up his other crimes as well, which included the 1977 beating of a Napa woman, an arrest for attempted oral copulation, and a six-month-to-life prison sentence for kidnapping a Hayward woman at knifepoint.

In fact, had the Petaluma Police Department not been worried about the press, Rankin and Howard might have stopped Davis right there. Although the Petaluma Police Department did issue a kidnapping bulletin within minutes of the crime, the police teletype carried the warning: "Not for Press Release." Those four words prevented some surrounding law enforcement agencies from broadcasting the information to patrol cars over unscrambled police channels throughout Sonoma County and other parts of the Bay Area. Rankin and Howard never knew about the Petaluma case.

As it turned out, an expansive radio alert was not sent out until 12:14 A.M.—about ninety minutes after the abduction. But once again fate took a cruel turn. The call did not go out on every available radio frequency. Howard and Rankin, who at that very moment were frisking Davis for weapons, were listening to a different radio channel. They didn't know how big a fish they had landed.

But on Pythian Road, Rankin and Howard had their work cut out for them. Howard shone a flashlight in Davis's eyes checking his pupils for any evidence of drugs or alcohol. Davis was sober, so he didn't flinch when the deputies looked into his car and noticed a six-pack of unopened 12-ounce Budweisers. Davis, calm and cocky as ever, reached into the car and opened one of the aluminum beer cans, right in front of the cops. He was about to toast his good fortune when Rankin told him to put the beer away. Still defiant, Davis tossed the can into a bush. Rankin told him to pick the trash up and place the empty in his car.

Howard noticed that brush and pine needles dotted Davis's thick head of hair. The sweat and dirt fitted with Davis's story that he had gotten stuck, then messed his clothes trying to dig his Pinto out of the ditch. Although the whole thing looked odd to the deputies, without a warrant or a citizen's arrest from Jaffe for trespassing, there was little they could do besides order Davis on his way.

But he didn't have enough money for a tow truck and didn't belong to American Automobile Association. Davis asked for their help.

The deputies tried to push the Pinto free with their shoulders while Davis gunned the engine, but there was not enough traction. Eventually, the deputies came up with a plan and borrowed a chain from Jaffe. They lashed it to the Pinto's bumper and used Howard's patrol car to free the trapped car. The men followed Davis as he backed out of Jaffe's steep driveway. The little episode seemed complete, but Davis tempted fate again. This time he stopped his car near a fork in the road just a short distance down the hill from where he had been stranded. He got out of the car. Rankin turned on his car's public address system and told Davis to move it.

"He kind of shrugged his shoulders, got back in his car and proceeded down Pythian Road toward Highway 12," Rankin said.

They escorted him to the bottom of the hill toward Highway 12, then went off to deal with an urgent call about a drive-by shooting.

As he sat inside the Pinto on the shoulder of Highway 12, Davis must have been stunned at his good fortune. Just two hours earlier he had broken into a stranger's home, scooped up a small child and made a clean getaway. He had just stared down two deputies and was free once more. All that remained was to tie up a few loose ends.

Four

THE HUNT FOR POLLY KLAAS

"From the outset, the reporters thought she was dead."

Marc Klaas had devoted his life to his only child. He spent every weekend with Polly and no matter where Eve Nichol moved the family, Marc was always nearby, picking her up from school on Friday and returning her for class on Monday. Marc had always loved children. Even at an early age, Marc showed a great interest in little ones. Marc was a teen-ager when his mother, B.J., became pregnant with her youngest child, Elizabeth, and when Joe Klaas broke the news to his son, the dutiful boy shared his mother's joy. "Mommy, you're the luckiest person in the world," Marc said.

Born April 11, 1949 in Anchorage, Alaska, Marc had a wandering childhood. His family bounced around California and Washington state. Joe Klaas moved the brood to Guadalajara, Mexico when Marc was a schoolboy. Marc attended a bilingual school, but ended up converting all his friends to the English language, Joe Klaas said.

Like his father, Marc took an interest in writing, but at a young age he showed an interest in the air force. He was ready to go until he grew disenchanted with the Vietnam War, Joe Klaas said. Instead, Marc spent the war years serving as a medical corpsman in Texas. He next ventured across the world and worked on a kibbutz in Israel.

After sweating it out on a collective farm in the Sinai, Marc signed up for school in New Delhi, India. Politics got in the way of his studies, however, when Indian leader Indira Gandhi capped American enrollment in national universities. Marc was stranded and lived like a beggar.

"He spent the last of his money on a train to Bombay," Joe Klaas remembered. "I kept trying to find a way to get money to him, but nothing could get through."

Joe Klaas said his son was destitute, living with a holy man in the streets. When he finally managed to get a plane ticket and $50 to his stranded son, the holy man disappeared, along with a bag Marc had left with the man for safekeeping.

"Marc went off to seek the spiritual answers to everything and he came back saying they did not know the answers in India. He got dysentery and to this day he can't even watch a movie about India," Joe Klaas said.

He tasted that same sense of wonder and fulfillment when Polly came into the world inside a San Francisco hospital on January 3, 1981. Marc and Eve divorced two years later, but the separation did not hinder his relationship with Polly. Father and daughter acted like best friends. "They were ga-ga for each other," Joe Klaas recalled. "I've never seen anything like it. She was the light of his life."

An hour or so after midnight on Oct. 2, 1993, Marc was at home inside the Sausalito, California condo he shared with his longtime girlfriend, Violet Cheer, when the call came that changed his life. Polly was missing. While other parents might freeze up, lost in fear and confusion, Marc took action. He snapped into gear and contacted the FBI in San Francisco.

FBI special agent Mark Mershon got the alarming news at about 6:30 A.M. on October 2. A graduate of Notre Dame, Mershon had planned to spend the day watching the Fighting Irish take on Stanford's football team in nearby Palo Alto. By the time he received a briefing on the investigation, twelve FBI agents were already examining evidence in Polly's house. He arranged for a friend to take his family to the football game, placed his ticket to the event in the sun visor of his Chevrolet Caprice in case Polly turned up, and drove north to Petaluma.

The twenty-year FBI veteran headed the bureau's Bay Area violent crimes division. He had grown up near Flemington, N.J., where Bruno Richard Hauptmann was convicted for kidnapping Charles Lindbergh's baby in 1935. The officer's parents often spoke about the famous abduction case, and now Mershon found himself in the middle of a similar nightmare.

As he absorbed the early facts about Polly's vanishing, Mershon thought about Amber Swartz Garcia, Michaela Joy Garecht, Elene Mischeloff and Nikki Campbell. These four young girls had all vanished without a trace from Bay Area communities in the past five years. Garcia, an eight-year-old from Pinole, California, had vanished on June 3, 1988 while jumping rope in front of her home. Nine-year-old Garecht disappeared from her Hayward, California home on November 19, 1988. She was last seen riding a scooter near a corner market. Mischeloff, thirteen, was abducted on January 30, 1989 while walking near school in Dublin, California. Campbell, age four, disappeared in December 1991 while playing outside her home in Fairfield, California.

Though he had worked ransom kidnapping cases in the past, the Klaas investigation was the first time he had taken on a stranger abduction case. The vast majority of those cases had ended badly with the victim dead or gone forever. Mershon was keenly aware of those crimes and did not want Polly Klaas's name added to the roll call of missing kids.

"I had personal resolve not to let that happen on my watch," he said.

Mershon was familiar with Petaluma since he had once considered moving there before settling in the East Bay. He had never been inside the police department, but knew that small town cops grow edgy when the feds arrive to help with a case. Mershon reasoned teamwork would be needed to get through the grueling investigation to come. He had his speech ready when he walked into Parks's office and introduced himself.

Chaos greeted him as he breezed through the front door of the police station. A mini command center had sprung up. FBI agents and cops worked side by side grabbing for phones and note pads. He braced himself, half expecting to butt heads with the local cops over a turf battle.

"I thought, 'here we go, this guy [Parks] will have a stereotype about the FBI, like we are the varsity and he is the junior varsity,'" Mershon said.

Instead, he and Parks forged a quick friendship that would carry both teams through the case. Together they set the rules which their departments would follow. Mershon knew that sixteen-hour days, fatigue, stress, and frustration would likely follow. He laid it on the line for everyone.

"Polly is our client," Mershon said.

When Pat Parks arrived at work at 9:00 A.M. on October 2, 1993, the place was overflowing with uniformed officers and G-men in suits and dark sunglasses. Petaluma's sleepy little cop shop had become the command center for the nation's largest man hunt. Parks next headed out to the crime scene and tried to place himself in the mind of the man responsible for this terrible act.

Parks is a slender man with thin, almost transparently blond hair. His face is ashen, narrow and bony. His voice is soft and assuring. He is a religious person, but he knows the evil that men can do. In his spare time Parks works as a hostage negotiator and specializes in efforts to free missionaries taken captive in all points of the globe. He had all the tools to show the Klaas family that there was a face behind the badge, that cops were regular guys too, that they had children, went to church and would bust their necks cracking the case.

As he pulled his car in front of Eve Nichol's home, he noticed the leaves on the elm tree that stood in the front yard had begun to change. He took note of the home's modest furnishings, its small kitchen and the games and toys that said this was a place with children. He felt at home in Eve Nichol's bungalow.

Eve Nichol sat on a living room couch when Parks arrived. Her eyes were filled with soul and sorrow. Her lips quivered.

"She asked if I had kids," Parks recalled.

As he stared into Eve's brown eyes, Parks wanted to guarantee her that Petaluma's finest were with her. But he didn't want to plant false hope.

"I got close to her and said, 'We will find your little girl,'" Parks recalled. "I was careful not to say 'we will bring her home,' because even then I had to allow that Polly may be dead."

Next, he moved to Polly's room and tried to think like a predator. He hoped the surroundings might lend clues to what the abductor had seen or had been thinking when he brought havoc to Fourth Street. The bedroom was dimly lit.

While Parks focused on the family, doing his best to calm their nerves, another man was doing his part to find Polly.

Bill Rhodes did not fit the role of a local hero, but the Petaluma Pip Printing shop owner with snow white hair and mustache had already taken command of an army of volunteers who had learned about the abduction that morning and gravitated to his copy shop in downtown Petaluma where printing machines were rolling off posters that carried Polly's picture.

Warren Salmons was standing outside Petaluma's downtown post office collecting money for a fund to help blind kids that morning when he first heard about Polly Klaas. The kidnapping was eleven hours old and already hundreds of flyers featuring a grinning twelve-year-old and a police drawing of her bushy-faced abductor were up all over town. By morning, it seemed half the community had gathered outside Rhodes's Pip Printing store just a few blocks away from where Salmons collected change.

Petaluma architect Dick Lieb saw his first Polly flyer the morning after the kidnapping. Like most longtime residents, he was shocked at the crime and joined in the hunt.

"We were all numb about this whole thing," Lieb said. "That some young girl was taken out of her house. We feel your house is a place you won't be bothered."

Over the next several weeks, thousands of volunteers mailed out flyers, collected information from phone tips and raised money to keep what would become The Polly Klaas Center alive.

Parks stopped by the copy center that day, amazed at how many people had gathered to help. He guessed there were at least a hundred people outside the store by mid-morning. Someone in authority needed to speak to them, to make sure they went about their searches properly. He was proud of his community, pleased that so many others had felt the same sense of duty toward the missing girl. Within a few weeks of the kidnapping, Rhodes had helped make more than 100,000 flyers. "Polly Power" had taken Petaluma by storm.

The Pip Printing store was charged with energy. Volunteers were everywhere, phones rang, hope swelled.

"We have high quality people here," Rhodes said at the time. "They are like angels, dropping in from the sky."

As time passed, people raised money for the search center through bake sales. Twenty-five phone lines were brought into the volunteer center. Some folks left casseroles or plates of cookies for the army of searchers. One little girl gave $5 to the cause and stuffed it in a donation jar by the center's front door.

"The heart of Petaluma is on fire for the love of this child," Rhodes said.

More than seven million kidnap flyers would eventually be mailed out across the country. One volunteer downloaded the flyers onto computers, then devised a way to send the images over cyberspace, spreading the story to more than twenty million on-line computer users.

"We hear stories of abductions where the child was found ten months later healthy and relatively whole," Rhodes told "America's Most Wanted." "Why can't this be one of those?"

But "Polly Power" and the hope of volunteers could only do so much. Professionals were needed to bring Polly back. The effort was amazing, but early on the volunteers and authorities relied on what turned out to be poor information. Some of the initial reports about the kidnapping were well off the mark. Neighbors told police they spotted a gray car in the area. They described it as a four-door Honda or Accord with primer paint on the doors and left front fender. One press account stated a similar car had been seen five miles away in Cotati two weeks earlier where a man in a blond wig and heavy makeup was reported to be approaching young girls.

The town was growing nervous. The media were buzzing all around. Some members of the press actually hid in the bushes near Polly's school to get interviews. Polly Klaas had become a national spectacle. To stave off the cameras and keep the media circus limited, Parks arranged to have Police Sgt. Mike Kerns, a beefy-looking but benevolent veteran officer, take charge of the press. Kerns was a good public speaker with a commanding build and booming voice. When he spoke up, people tended to listen.

As day two of the crisis ended, Parks shared a pesto dinner with Mershon. Parks was happy to have the FBI's help. The bureau had deep pockets, access to elaborate data bases, and the latest technology to pick out valuable evidence like unseen fingerprints and hair or carpet fibers the kidnapper might have left behind. The FBI could also put more investigators into the field.

Before Polly Klaas captured the nation's attention, there had not been a murder in town for more than two years. But the police force had not grown since 1986, even though the city's population expanded at a steady rate. The town's 54-person police force had dealt with murders and child sex cases, but on average the city has only one big crime every two years or so. It was hardly the best time for the worst crime in city history to take place.

"Our organization had come into this situation on the verge of a crisis," Parks said, referring to his overworked officers and the lack of faith they had for management. "Now we were dead in the middle of one."

By that Sunday, 50,000 flyers had been sent out and posted in every store in

Petaluma and in most every shop window in
surrounding towns. Polly's face was everywhere. And fear was creeping into the minds
of a town that had barely experienced violent crime. Parents did not let young children out at night. School kids were driven
to campus and picked up after class by
frightened adults. Daughters did not venture
far from home without escorts.

"I've got a son who slept in a family room
last night with the lights on," Petaluma resident Sharon North told the *San Jose Mercury
News.* "He is 6 feet tall and weighs 195
pounds."

North's daughter, Kristen, was one of
more than a hundred people who gathered
in front of the Petaluma Community Center
Sunday night and prayed.

"I think this will help," Kristen North told
the *Mercury News.* "I have a feeling she
would know people are thinking about her."

Almost immediately, rumors about satanic
cults, and advice from mystics poured in
from tipsters. The first "left field" shocker
came twenty-four hours after the abduction,
when a teen-aged girl, who sounded just like
Polly, called Marc Klaas's home claiming to
be his daughter. The mystery girl said she
was being held in a hotel room and that her
abductor had gone out for a few minutes before the line went dead.

A frantic effort ensued as FBI agents

culled the toll lines to locate the caller. At the time, Marc Klaas's phone was not set up for a trace, so the cops could not track the mystery girl. When she phoned again ten days later, police traced the call and sent officers out to give the prankster a lesson in civics and police work. The girl said she had done the deed on a dare.

"It was an extremely painful moment," Mershon recalled.

The call had provided a moment of hope, but when the truth came everyone sagged with disappointment.

Next came talk about a devil-worshiping cult that snatched Polly for unknown and evil purposes. After that, Eve's husband, Allan Nichol, demanded the Petaluma cops check out a lead he got from a psychic. Parks wanted to look into the mystic's premonition, not because he trusted the unknown psychic, but because he wanted to appease Nichol and get close to Polly's stepfather. It was no secret that Polly and Allan Nichol had had some disputes.

"At first there had been allegations that Polly and Allan did not get along and that maybe she had run away because of that," Parks said.

The top brass did not want Parks searching a field in Napa on the say-so of some psychic. They canceled the idea, but Parks eventually got to know Allan Nichol and established a good rapport.

At Polly's junior high school, terror became the only subject worth studying. By Monday, all of Polly's classmates at Petaluma Junior High had heard the news. Many had spent part of the weekend searching for their missing friend. Now it was time to face the media, encamped outside the three-acre site that housed 800 youngsters. No one knew if the suspect would show up at school to snatch another child.

"There was a lot of fear," recalled Petaluma Junior High School Assistant Principal Joel Baum. "Kids were really scared. They did not know who did this or if they were still running around. There was a lot of concern for Polly and whether she was going to be OK."

This was Baum's first year in Petaluma. "It was a pretty tough entrance to the town," he said.

Baum kept a picture of Polly in his office throughout the crisis. He said that what happened to little Polly forever changed most of the middle school students in attendance. Many showed up late for classes for the rest of the year. Some homework assignments never got done. Kids lost sleep. Counselors were brought in to help the seventh and eighth graders cope. Self-defense classes were offered and highly attended.

"There was a great deal of fear here because no one knew how this would end," Baum said. "There would be peaks of hope, then the hope would be dashed and the wound would be reopened."

Rumors spread through campus. It was said that Polly had phoned her parents, that her kidnapper had been following her for three days, and that the missing girl's clothing had been found in a trash can. Counselors advised parents to play it straight with their kids and acknowledge their own fears. Through it all, the campus became a family. The students made a quilt with messages to Polly. A "Pennies for Polly" fund-raiser got started, and kids distributed purple ribbons in honor of Polly's favorite color. The quilt became good therapy for the stressed student population. One student stitched a yin-yang symbol for the missing twelve-year-old.

"What goes around comes around, you're going to be OK and he [the abductor] is going to suffer," Emily Lauere told the *Santa Rosa Press Democrat* when asked why she put the karmic symbol into the quilt.

Kids even put big yellow ribbons around the desk Polly used—to honor the missing girl.

"This was a real difficult period for us," Baum said. "Polly was a real light. A lot of teachers said when she spoke in class, the kids paid attention. She had a special light about her that drew people in."

"There was probably no one in the world who hated her," seventh grader Trisha Stetch told the *Santa Rosa Press Democrat* after she tied the ribbon around Polly's desk in their history class. "She was the nicest person."

Even teachers were shattered.

"My teacher was crying," twelve-year-old Vanessa Magnani told the Santa Rosa paper three days after the kidnapping. "It was real sad."

"We're thinking what we are going to do is try a reward," Stetch told the *Press Democrat*. "We're never going to stop trying."

But all the hype did not affect Davis, who had since returned to his halfway house, called Turning Point, in San Mateo and carried on with his life. He continued to work at a sheet metal shop, and chatted with fellow travelers at the home for wayward adults as if nothing out of the ordinary had ever taken place. Folks inside the transitional home teased him a bit. A few joked that he looked a little like the white guy depicted on those wanted posters that had appeared across the Bay Area and occasionally popped up on newscasts. One guy quipped that Davis should make sure the missing twelve-year-old got some food.

The career convict had arrived at Turning Point only ninety days before, following his parole from state prison. He had been tense from the start. Davis has spent the majority of his life behind bars. He had become institutionalized and had trouble adjusting to life on the outside. He told a few friends inside the home that he planned to go out in a blaze of glory with police.

But most people inside Turning Point did not know of Davis's violent background and brushed off his odd remarks and promises to commit a real sensational crime. Many residents took him for a typical con, a guy full of talk who would say anything to manipulate others while trying to find a way to bend the rules.

While the Petaluma police and FBI agents ran down rumors that always led to dead ends, Davis played it cool and continued to make regular visits to his sister and brother-in-law in Ukiah. The travel route took him past Petaluma and by a thicket of brush just outside the town of Cloverdale.

"Whenever Rick was around it was like talking to anyone," Davis's brother-in-law Dick Schwarm said. "You could not tell he was violent or anything. All we did was sit around and talk."

Dick and Darlene Schwarm were inside their rental home on an Indian reservation just outside of Ukiah when they learned of the kidnapping. They had heard the news on television. Soon flyers with the missing child and her abductor began appearing all over Ukiah. Davis visited the family in late October. He watched television with them and played with their four kids, who considered Rick the perfect uncle. While staying at the Schwarm home, Rick Davis helped his brother-in-law strip down cars. He had no reaction to news reports as he sat on the family couch and watched television with his relatives.

Just eighteen days after the kidnapping, Davis was picked up for drunken driving by a CHP officer in Ukiah, but officers there never connected him with the crime and let him out of jail. They were not the only ones to look into Davis's face and miss the connection. Dick Schwarm said he and Davis traveled across Sonoma County in November checking for auto parts. They drove to a shopping center in Santa Rosa that was littered with flyers about the famous kidnapping, then drove through Petaluma. No one paid Davis any mind. Meanwhile, attention turned toward another suspect.

About two weeks after the kidnapping, James Arthur Heard, Jr. phoned the

Petaluma Police Department claiming he could guarantee Polly's safe return in exchange for $10,000. He told authorities he would harm the girl if his instructions for a money drop were not followed. Authorities said the money would be waiting for him beneath a bus stop bench, but no one showed up for the cash.

Authorities traced one of Heard's ransom demand phone calls to a Petaluma apartment not far from the bus stop drop point. They went after him full force. SWAT officers and FBI agents in war gear smashed into his apartment with their guns drawn.

"I think he was scared to death," Parks said.

They cuffed Heard immediately, then quickly realized he was not the man who took Polly. Still, the message had been given that police would not tolerate any cranks interested in cashing in on another family's tragedy. The cops felt good about taking this joker out of the equation. It was a bright moment in an otherwise dark story. Sgt. Kerns called the extortion attempt "stupid," especially because by that time a $200,000 reward had been posted by Winona Ryder.

Heard, a twenty-year-old nurse's assistant, pleaded no contest to charges and received a sentence of six months in jail.

Weeks later, a second man tried the same scam. By then the authorities were so busy tracking more solid leads they didn't bother to arrest the fraud. Instead, they knocked on his door and told him to knock it off. But the energy that the media called "Polly Power" continued to grow, even as hopes among the media and the police department began to fade. Within two weeks of the crime, Polly's name and face were not only all over the computer Internet, but on "Eye to Eye" with Connie Chung. Two thousand tips had been called in to Petaluma and an army of 1,200 volunteers had spent time searching every field and ditch for miles around the city.

But, still, there was no sign of Polly Klaas. "The cops were exhausted and exhilarated," said *Santa Rosa Press Democrat* reporter Randi Rossman, who covered Petaluma at the time and had sources inside the Petaluma Police Department. "A lot of them put their whole life into this case. There were a lot of valiant efforts, heroic stuff, but there was some grandstanding too."

Rossman had just come off maternity leave after giving birth to a boy and was assigned to the paper's Petaluma bureau when the crisis hit. Like the local cops, she would put in fourteen-hour days and then got tips at home. As the case grew and the town became home to a massive media circus, Rossman worked her sources and watched them put up a good front until the television lights dimmed.

"It was cheerleading every day [by the police]," Rossman said. " 'We'll get her,' they would say. Behind the scenes they felt she was dead, because that is how it usually works. From the outset, the reporters felt she was dead."

But others held out for the best.

"Everyone had all this hope, everyone was so positive," recalled Maureen Dixon, a volunteer who joined the Polly Klaas Center days after the abduction. "The mood was always positive. I don't think we could have come to the center unless we really thought we could get her back. If that happened to my children, I would want the whole world out there. I wanted to set an example that for one child it is worth putting out seven million flyers. Every single child is worth that effort."

By mid-October, Petalumans were making efforts toward better home security. Hardware stores and alarm companies began doing big business as locals got security conscious for the first time in their lives. The interest in home security was based not only on the Klaas case, but because the town had suffered its first drive-by shooting two weeks before Davis broke into Polly's home. Deadbolts, window locks and flip latches for doors became hot items.

"We had a couple of people come in asking for tear gas," Big Five Sporting Goods store assistant manager, Kevin Cook, told the Santa Rosa newspaper. "Basically, the awareness [that] it can happen in towns like this is definitely scaring people."

The pressure was mounting for Sonoma County authorities. Though volunteers had been beating the brush and tracking phone tips, no good leads had yet been found. It was time for the cops to take a deeper look at what the two young witnesses saw that night. Police gave Kate and Gillian a polygraph examination to circle in on what really happened the night Polly was taken. New details about the kidnapping emerged and the abductor's image began to take shape with the help of Jean Boylan, a well-known forensic artist from Bend, Oregon. Her unique blend of therapy and artistry earned her a national reputation with the FBI. She spent time with Kate and Gillian and emerged with a new composite drawing. This one was far more vivid than the one that had floated around for weeks.

Boylan, who has drawn suspect pictures for fourteen years on 7,000 cases, takes a different approach from that of the police officers who rely on her work. While most police sketch artists show witnesses catalogues of various eyes, noses and mouths, and ask them to pick the features that resemble the criminal, Boylan probes with kind words.

"This has nothing to do with art," she told the *Los Angeles Times,* when asked to describe her skills. "This is all about the interview, about the brain, how it processes memory and how trauma affects memory. The art is not the point. The point is to get accurate information. It is about developing a place of safety, listening skills, interview skills."

The new drawing was much different from the one first offered by police the day after Polly's abduction. In Boylan's version, the suspect had a thicker face, a darker complexion and thick wavy hair.

"It's a face," Marc Klaas said when the new sketch was produced. "It's a personality. I hope it has an immediate effect."

Five

BIG BREAK

"You think this is Polly?"

Nearly two months had passed since Polly's slumber party. The people of Petaluma had suffered through the peaks and valleys of what had become an exhausting story of grief and heartache. The highs came when a good tip emerged through the volunteer center. The lows quickly followed when the information led nowhere. Marc Klaas and Eve Nichol kept their faith through the strain. They felt Polly was alive, still captive under the menacing eye of the thick-chested and dark-faced intruder who had emerged like a ghost only to evaporate into the dark of night as quickly as he had come.

At the Pip Printing office, still the center of the volunteer search effort, people kept busy. They took phone tips, mailed out thousands of kidnap posters and comforted each other. Cynics in the press might have believed the worst had befallen the missing child, but the volunteers held tight to their fading hope. None wanted Polly's smiling face, her tantalizing eyes and soft brown hair to fade into memory. They did not want her lost among the ranks of those other kidnapped children who never return to the town and people who loved them.

The volunteers prayed for a break in the case. Instead, a blast from the past brought Bill Rhodes down in shame. The copy shop became the center of controversy after a thirty-two-year-old woman sued Rhodes and accused him of sexually molesting her more than twenty years before. The alleged victim, identified only as "Victoria Anne," claimed in a civil lawsuit that Rhodes had abused her in 1970 and 1971 when she was nine years old. Local newspapers reported Rhodes had been convicted of indecent exposure in 1968 and acquitted on charges of molesting several young girls at knifepoint that same year. He called the lawsuit "ridiculous" according to press accounts but added that he had joined the Klaas search effort to "make amends" for his past. The news stunned locals, and the volunteers searching for Polly.

In mid November 1993, Rhodes resigned as head of the search center he helped create. He denied knowing anyone named Victoria Anne and denied her allegations, according to the *Santa Rosa Press Democrat*. Petaluma police had been aware of the allegations against Rhodes early on. They had questioned him as a possible suspect but found no connection between him and the missing girl. Despite the controversy, Rhodes's contribution to the search for Polly will be long remembered.

"Bill Rhodes did the most to get this started," Joe Klaas said a year after Polly's abduction. "I will never stop being grateful to Bill Rhodes. He did one hell of a job."

Rhodes remained a popular figure to many in Petaluma even after the lawsuit became public. Listeners on a Sonoma County radio show voted him "top citizen" for his efforts in the Klaas case, according to the Santa Rosa paper. But Rhodes's dramatics only added more spice to the abduction saga. Stress was mounting, fingers were being pointed, and authorities were being blamed for failing to locate the child. Something had to break.

It came instead by accident when Dana Jaffe took a walk with two friends around her property. Like everyone else in Sonoma County, Jaffe was well aware of Polly's disappearance. But like so many others, she had not suspected the "scary looking" guy in the Pinto she had met on October 1 had any link to Polly's disappearance.

Jaffe and two friends strolled the land on November 27, 1993 checking out how much brush needed to be cleared for the upcoming fire season. They walked for some time and had cut across fire roads picking up debris like oil cans and garbage left by wood cutters. They climbed a steep section of land and struggled over the loose bark and leaves, only to find a bright object near the trunk of a tree. Jaffe's eyes shot to a pair of red tights. They looked like something little girls wore on cold nights.

The hikers spotted a man's size black sweatshirt laid out on the ground next to the tights. The leaves around the sweatshirt had been brushed away as if someone had sat there for a spell. Strips of binding tape and a knotted piece of cloth that was shaped like a hood lay nearby.

"The tights and the white pieces of cloth made me feel like they were really out of place," Jaffe said. "I didn't like the way they looked. They looked like they were ties or gags."

Jaffe asked her hiking partners, "Do you think this is Polly?"

It was then that Jaffe recalled the trespasser. She called the Sonoma County Sheriff's Department at about 5:00 P.M. that day, but left no message after reaching the station's answering machine. The next day she got a call from work and mentioned the unusual find to her boss. She figured a second call to the Sheriff's Department was in order. This time Jaffe reached Sheriff's Deputy Michael McManus, a twenty-one-year-veteran with the force, who had had a hand in many of the county's more notorious crimes.

A light rain fell when McManus drove up the road that leads to Jaffe's property. The call might have sounded a bit bland to other officers, but McManus, who had worked as K-9 (police dog) patrol officer and search and rescue specialist, wanted a closer look. He and Jaffe walked along a steep hill that led from her home. The territory was dotted with scrub oaks. Loose mulch from tree bark, fallen leaves and branches coated the ground. It was hard traveling. It was slippery.

"Not a place that a person out for a walk would go to," McManus said.

When they reached the tree trunk, McManus knew something was wrong. His police mind ticked off the facts as he scanned the scene. Everything about the placement of the garments looked suspicious. In addition to the dark sweatshirt, the girl's tights, the cloth pieces and two twelve- to eighteen-inch long strips of packaging tape, McManus found matches and an un-rolled Rough Rider condom on the ground.

"That leads you to believe there was an attempt or committed sexual assault most likely between a man and a little girl," McManus said. "You don't normally see little kids with condoms unless they use them for water balloons."

Another officer might not have taken such keen interest in checking out a call about a pair of tights, but McManus, always gung-ho,

charged ahead. He placed everything he saw
near the oak tree, except the condom, into
paper evidence bags. He left the condom to
mark the spot in case further investigation
was required. There was no need to worry
about contaminating the evidence. If the
condom contained any fluids or hairs, the
rubber itself would protect the material from
the rain. McManus took the bagged items to
the Sheriff's Department substation about
nine miles away from Pythian Road in a
community called Agua Caliente. He placed
the material on towels and notified detectives. Jaffe had already told McManus about
her encounter with Davis. McManus next
searched department records, found the trespassing report taken weeks before. He
looked up Davis's past record that was literally as long as a man's arm.

"Everything was snowballing," McManus
said. "Jaffe's call was a little pebble rolling
down a hill. By the time we called Petaluma
Police, the ball had gotten real big and we
were pretty sure what we had. Every time I
turned to something the pendulum was
swinging harder and faster."

He called Petaluma investigators and told
them about Davis's criminal past. They sped
away from Petaluma as if chasing a runaway
fire that was aimed toward a gas station.

Petaluma investigators took one look at the
tights and pieces of cloth and knew instantly

the fabric matched pieces used to tie up Kate and Gillian.

"They didn't spend thirty seconds looking at it," McManus said.

"When I looked at the evidence it all just clicked," said Petaluma Police Sgt. and lead investigator on the case Mike Meese. "If you stand there and look at it, it all makes sense."

The items were hand-delivered to an FBI specialist in Washington, D.C. Experts put the goods through microscopic review and struck gold. An analysis of the find confirmed what McManus and Meese thought to be true. The federal lab technicians determined the cloth items found at Pythian Road had been cut by scissors. The fragments found on the hillside matched perfectly with the fabric used to bind and gag the twelve-year-olds inside Polly's home. Further review picked up traces of threads that later matched to the brown carpet inside Davis's Pinto. The FBI also lifted bits of red material from the black sweatshirt left by the oak tree. The tiny bits of fabric matched the floral nightgown Gillian Pelham had brought to Polly's house that terrible night.

Mershon was at the base of Pythian Road the next day while search and rescue teams scoured the hillside for evidence. He was taking in the beautiful sunny day when his cellular phone sounded with word from

Washington that the evidence matched up. He swelled with pride. The lab boys had done well.

"When they say it's a match, it's a match," Mershon recalled. Just forty-eight hours after Jaffe stumbled onto the rag-tag items, the case was made.

Best of all, investigators now had prints to compare with the partial palm print lifted from a bunk bed inside Polly Klaas's bedroom. They matched with Davis.

"We knew we had our guy," Capt. Parks said. "It was good and bad news, good that we had identified him, bad because of what kind of person he was."

Police spokesman Mike Kerns rounded up the media to downplay a breaking story out of Riverside that indicated Polly's kidnapper was living there. The press conference distracted the newshounds and allowed police to bring Eve Nichol and Marc Klaas into the station unseen. The family gathered with Parks inside the police chief's office to get the news.

"Marc and I went to the police department and they informed us together they had identified the suspect," Nichol told "America's Most Wanted." "I asked is this a bad guy? They said, 'Yeah.' "

Marc was nervous, he wanted to know everything. His face was pale. He had the look of fear, worry and anger. Eve looked as if she had accepted the worst to be true. Marc shook with hostility when they told him about Davis's violent past.

In front of the station Kerns told reporters they were chasing wild geese in Riverside. Petaluma's lawmen mounted up. They were ready to end this thing.

"Everyone was watching Kerns," Parks said. "We waltzed out the other door."

Six

THE CONFESSION

"There were tears from him. How much was genuine . . . is a judgment call."

An impressive armada of FBI agents, police SWAT members, sheriff's deputies and Petaluma detectives rolled eighty miles north along Highway 101 to the Coyote Valley Indian Rancheria reservation just north of Ukiah. Their target: an ill-kept three-bedroom house where Richard Davis often stayed with his baby sister Darlene and her heavy-set husband Dick Schwarm. The Schwarms had rented the place from a member of the Pomo Indian tribe for two years. They made a living for themselves and their four kids tearing down cars on their property and selling junk. The place looked like the set from the old television comedy "Sanford and Son."

But there would be no laughter in the junkyard on November 30, when forty lawmen kicked in doors and ransacked the residence looking for Davis, Polly or clues to where either could be found. There were moments of panic because when the hell storm of lawmen descended on the junkyard home, the place was empty. The cops all hoped the target had not eluded them.

The remoteness of the Schwarm home made it impossible to watch Davis without tipping him off. The authorities did not want to be spotted and risk the chance of having Davis figure things out and turn rabbit. Instead, they dove in full force.

The stress quickly eased when Davis was seen driving behind his brother-in-law toward the home. Dick Schwarm was returning to his residence in a 1973 Grand Prix just ahead of his brother-in-law. Schwarm's two daughters, aged fourteen and seven, rode with Davis in a trailing Chevrolet van.

Mershon pointed toward Parks and Meese. They hopped in his car and moved in for the capture.

"This is it," Mershon thought to himself. Davis took it all in stride.

"He was totally calm," Mershon said.

The cops tried to stay calm too. They wanted this thing to go down easy.

"They asked who I was and who Rick was," Dick Schwarm said. "I thought they were picking Rick up for a parole violation."

All three investigators approached Davis's van.

"It was a very low-key arrest," Meese said. "He was sitting in his car smoking a cigarette. I walked up to the car, my gun hidden behind my leg. Pat asked him how he was doing and had Davis step out of the car."

Meese put the cuffs on Davis and said he was under arrest for violating parole as a result of an October 19 drunken driving charge. Meese traveled with Davis to the Mendocino County Courthouse in nearby Ukiah. The two made small talk, passing words between the mesh cage that separated cop from criminal inside the squad car. Meanwhile, FBI agents and other officers tore the Schwarms' home apart. Authorities found sixteen grams of methamphetamine in the home during the arrest and questioned Dick Schwarm for hours.

"They kicked in doors and busted open car trunks even after I said I would give them the keys," Dick Schwarm said. "They asked if I thought he [Rick] could have done it [the kidnapping]," Dick Schwarm said. "I told them I knew nothing about it."

Dick and Darlene Schwarm never made it back to their rental home. When news got out that the most notorious crime in county history was linked to the reservation, tribal elders suddenly remembered Dick and Darlene were not members of the tribe. They accused the Schwarms of squatting on the land and never let them return. Tribal leaders told the media the Schwarms' rental agreement lacked approval by the U. S. Department of Interior, which oversees Native

American matters. In Mendocino County, the Schwarms had become untouchables. Darlene lost her job at a school cafeteria. Their children were harassed.

"One kid asked my son how Rick liked her [Polly's] dying quivers," Darlene Schwarm said. "I told the school I would sue if that happened again. People can do what they want to me, but not my kids."

The family would live like nomads for the next eight months looking for a new place to call home. Whenever Dick Schwarm checked out an apartment or home advertised for rent, the landlord would say the place was already taken.

"They [the tribe] still look at us as if we did something wrong," Darlene said. "We did nothing wrong. We had no idea anything was going wrong. . . . They never had any trouble with us before this, now we are blackballed because of what my brother did."

Meanwhile, Davis kept patient inside his Mendocino County jail cell. The cops and FBI agents kept busy too, sifting through the evidence and slowly building a case. Kate and Gillian were taken to identify the suspect. Newspaper reports stated other witnesses near Polly's house recognized Davis as the stranger seen lurking on Fourth Street the night she was abducted. On December 2, 1993, Davis appeared in court to answer for his DUI arrest. The suspect was flanked by Mendocino County Sheriff James Ruso and several deputies. Davis slouched in a chair during the five-minute hearing. His heavy beard was gone. A thick mustache with flakes of gray framed his sealed lips.

"Yep," he said when asked if he wanted to plead guilty to the drunken driving charge before being whisked off for a thirty-day sentence. Davis barely stirred for the horde of reporters. His heavily tattooed arms, which carry the images of a peacock and the Grim Reaper, were exposed for all to see. Outside the court, Davis did not turn away from the cameras. He told his guards to slow their pace. "My feet don't move that fast," according to the *Santa Rosa Press Democrat*.

"Did you take Polly?" one reporter asked. Davis did not reply.

As yet, there was no official connection between Davis and Polly Klaas, but everyone suspected the tattooed con was good for the crime and figured it was a matter of time before the hammer fell. Students remained jittery at Polly's junior high school. They were happy to have the prime suspect jailed but afraid of what lay ahead.

"Where's Polly," a seventh-grader repeatedly chanted to himself, according to an account in the *San Jose Mercury News*.

A senior at the town's high school didn't believe Polly would come home alive. "It's been too much time," he told the *Mercury News*. "The young generations, we've seen a lot of stuff happen. Most of us don't want to get our hopes up."

Petaluma Police Chief Dennis DeWitt stayed positive, at least for the cameras. He said there was a chance Polly was alive. His words brought cheers from volunteers at the Polly Klaas Center in Petaluma, left shaken upon seeing the true face of the man whose likeness appeared on millions of flyers they had mailed across the world.

"I am very happy we've got a suspect in view," volunteer Robin Thomas told the Santa Rosa paper. "I hope it will turn out that he's our man, that he tells us where Polly is, and that she'll be home for Christmas."

While Davis held still in the growing storm, deputies and search dogs scoured Pythian Road looking for additional clues. Helicopters with heat-seeking devices criss-crossed above the hilly landscape as night fell. Fifty volunteers combed the land and fanned out over a three-mile-wide zone. Divers searched two reservoirs and a water tower. Bill Rivas, a neighbor of Dana Jaffe, lamented a lost opportunity to help. Rivas told the press that Jaffe had alerted him to her October 1 encounter with the trespasser. Rivas said neither he nor Jaffe contacted authorities about their early suspicions because they assumed the sheriffs who confronted Davis two months before had already checked out the trespasser.

Three days after Davis's arrest, the palm print match became public news. The print put him inside the house. It was a critical piece of evidence. The print, the eyewitness identification and fibers taken from the items found at Pythian Road were the building blocks of a strong case against Davis. But the prime suspect remained silent, invoking his Miranda rights.

"He will not be questioned any further," said Sonoma County District Attorney Gene Tunney.

But Davis had always been a talker. His legacy of crimes almost always came with a confession of some type. The cops waited for Davis to blink. The breakdown came four days after his arrest when a friend who worked with Davis at a San Mateo sheet metal shop visited the suspect in jail and told him the cops had found a palm print and were closing in. It was only a matter of time before they charged him with kidnapping. Davis needed to try and control the situation before the law boxed him in for good. It was time to talk. He used a jailhouse phone and contacted Meese.

Following the arrest, several detectives had

come before Davis, each trying in their own
way to win his confidence or get him to
loosen up. Most had been hard-nosed. They
tossed their business cards at him, but Davis
was not impressed. Only Meese had been low
key. He kept his business cards off the table.
Davis responded to the soft touch.

By now, Polly had been gone more than
two months. Meese figured the pretty youngster was dead, but he had to hear it from
Davis first.

"I asked if we could go and get Polly,"
Meese said. "He told me, 'No' and from the
choice of his words and the tone of his voice,
I knew she was dead."

Meese didn't care what the man wanted to
say, just so long as he got it all down for
the record. Meese raced from the search
zone by Jaffe's house and sped toward
Davis's holding cell. A video camcorder was
readied to take Davis's confession. Meese figured Davis was ready to talk because he had
no other alternative. By confessing, he had
some control. Meese played it straight with
Davis as the men sat inside an interview
room at the Mendocino County Sheriff's Department. Meese read Davis his rights and
told him anything he said could be used
against him in court. Davis signed a form
indicating that he was speaking freely.

"When he learned about the palm print
he knew we had him," Meese said. "The

case stands alone with just the physical evidence. Now he wanted to control the paint brush and make a picture."

Davis confessed. He said he had strangled the girl, then told investigators where they could find Polly's body.

"He said somebody could find her, in fact he was surprised that nobody had discovered her yet, or that no one had smelled anything yet," Meese said.

Davis turned misty-eyed as if he felt sorry for all he had done.

"There were tears from him," Meese said. "I took it for what it was and tried to make it so he was in a position where he would talk. How much of his tears were genuine or self serving is a judgment call. This was the way he chose to display himself."

Meese touched Davis in a sign of support, but Davis wanted no pity.

"I patted him on the back and he said, 'You know, [you] ain't got to show me no consideration, or no respect. I know I'm a piece of shit.' "

They talked for almost ten hours, Davis, in his gruff, deep voice, giving up more and more details as the time dragged on. He told Meese he came to town to find his mother, he ran into the old bum who sold him PCP-laced marijuana, how he suddenly found Polly inside his car. And finally, how he killed her with a swift jerk of the neck.

Sonoma County prosecutor Greg Jacobs was not moved by Davis's video passion play.

"It is hard to say if the emotion on the tape is for doing the crime or for being caught," Jacobs said. "I think it is remorse over the fact he has brought this whole thing down on himself, not because he feels sorry. There are parts of the tape where he is callous and calls Polly, 'a broad.' He keeps saying, 'I fucked up.' He never says that this is a terrible thing. It is more like this was stupid, like he didn't need to go this far. The description of the strangulation is very, very cold."

How much of what Davis said is true and how much is an effort to put some kind of beneficial spin out for himself is not known. All Meese knows is that the description of Polly's death matches the evidence. Polly's case would be the forty-year-old cop's career highlight and his first criminal investigation in three years. Forty-two large, spool notebooks line a wall in his office. All contain bits and pieces about the case. Though he had previously worked with the SWAT team and investigated child molestation cases, Meese spent the past few years in personnel hiring new recruits. He had worked only two other homicides during his thirteen years with the police department.

"I'm a small-town cop," he said.

Meese began his career as a military police

officer while stationed in Germany in 1973. His first murder investigation centered on the stabbing death of a nuclear missile battery commander who discovered a stash of marijuana in his company's barracks. Four men were convicted of killing the commander to protect a pound of pot. Meese is a controlled man who watches what he says and listens carefully to others. He prefers a quiet stream to city life and loves the intricate details of an investigation. He keeps a cabin near Redding, California that he built himself and retreats there for peace.

"When I talked to Davis, I tried to treat him as a human being and give him the respect he was entitled, without taking away from what he did and without adding any more degradation. I set my emotions aside and treated him as a person. Had I gone in and acted like the almighty cop, with mirrored sunglasses, I don't think he would have talked. When I got there it was one person talking to another."

The men spent hours in Ukiah, but later traveled to Petaluma where Davis continued his story. Meese had grown close to Marc Klaas and Eve Nichol. He wanted to milk Davis for all he could. He wanted to find the girl's body. He didn't want Polly to be one of those kids seen on the sides of milk cartons— the children who everyone suspects are dead, but remain forever missing, leaving their families with an emptiness that can never be filled; a wound that can never be closed.

"I have kids of my own and I can understand how you can become enraged with such a case," Meese said. "But that would not have solved anything. I did not have time to let my personal feelings get in the way. Now when I watch the video, I am amazed I could sit there and listen to what he says and the tone of his voice."

The long investigation had left Meese shaken. He had come to look at Polly as one of his own. He had read her school work, watched her on video tapes, listened to her voice. He had read her diary, sat in her bedroom, and held her clothes.

"People say police don't get emotionally involved, but that is bullshit," Meese said. "That is why you work twenty-four hours a day on a case like this and not fall over dead. I would go home each night at 4 a.m. and the first thing I would do is wake my kids up just so I could hold them."

After telling his tale, Davis was ready to lead the cops to Polly. Meese, Davis and Larry Taylor, an FBI agent and behavioral specialist, traveled along Highway 101 in an unmarked Mendocino County Sheriff's Department car in the late afternoon. Meese knew what to expect, but part of him didn't really want to know it all, as they exited

Highway 101 near Cloverdale and traveled on a side road that led to a structure of rotting wood buildings that stood out just off the highway near a side road. Twenty years before, the place was a working saw mill. On busy days, the surrounding hills were covered in sawdust. Now the spot was forgotten and deserted, save for a cone-shaped processing burner made of steel and wire mesh. From a distance, the rust-colored burner looked like an ancient mound that might hide a buried Mayan pyramid. The discarded metal and mesh monolith had stood witness to the atrocity.

Davis turned quiet as the car rolled off the shoulder and stopped on a dirt patch fifty yards from a thick stand of bushes, berries and weeds. The entire mood inside the car changed. An ominous flow of human energy had overtaken the car. Davis stopped smoking and pointed toward the weeds. Sonoma County District Attorney investigator Mike Griffith, who had followed the men, walked toward the berry bushes, while Davis and Meese stood outside their car. It was dusk and Griffith searched with a flashlight.

"This is it," Griffith said as the beam caught something beneath a layer of plywood. They found Polly lying on her back. Her skull had separated from the body. A knotted piece of rope lay tangled in her hair. The flannel nightgown she wore over her clothes that night had been pulled up to her chest. The pink shirt she had worn tied at the midriff was undone. Her hands rested on top of one another. Her white miniskirt had been pulled up from the bottom. Her feet were separated and her knees. Davis stood quiet as investigators walked around the body.

"Davis didn't say anything," Meese said. "We put him back in the car and cuffed him. The ride south was somber."

The position of the body, coupled with Davis's past crimes and the unrolled condom found at Pythian Road led investigators to suspect Polly had been raped or at least molested before death.

Inside the Petaluma Police Department, Capt. Parks faced a tougher duty. He had to break the news to Polly's family. Parks didn't want to handle the task alone. After learning that Polly's body had been found, he called his friend, FBI agent Mershon, in San Francisco and asked him to come north to Petaluma. Mershon's family was having a Christmas party, but he left the festival to be at his partner's side.

Mershon let Parks talk to his wife. She quickly agreed to let him leave the party and do his duty. He raced off to Petaluma and prepared himself for the worst. Death notifications do not normally fall on the shoulders of FBI agents, but Mershon had carried

this case too long to let the detail fall to anyone else. He, like so many other officers
linked to the tragedy, had become a foster
parent to Polly. From the start of the case
he knew the chances of getting her back
alive were slim. Now the game was over and
the news had to be delivered quickly, but
with compassion.

Parks called Marc Klaas in Sausalito and
told him to stop by the station.

"He asked if there was anything he needed
to know and it was the first time I ever lied
to him," Parks said. "I said, 'No, I just want
to talk to you.'"

The four gathered inside the station. Eve
sat across from Parks. Marc was across from
Mershon. Everyone sat within hand holding
distance.

"We broke it not abruptly, but very frankly,"
Parks said.

Mershon told them that Davis had confessed to the murder. Emotion gripped his
throat. He choked up. Everyone else went to
pieces.

"All the anger came out of Marc. Only one
week earlier we had tried to break him to the
possibility of bad news and he accused us of
practically stealing Christmas," Parks said.
"This day he was in rage, justifiable rage. He
pounded his fists and slumped in the chair."

Mershon spread the news to Marc's girlfriend Violet Cheer and Joe Klaas. The

grandfather, who had stood throughout the crisis like a defiant tower, convinced his grandchild had been taken as part of an elaborate conspiracy, sank in grief.

"It was like the air went out of him. He said, 'I never thought it would end like this,' " Mershon said.

"It is with unspeakable sorrow that I must let go of the dream we all shared—the dream of our sweet Polly coming home again," Eve Nichol said. "My heart tells me that she is in a place filled with light and love."

For sixty-four days, Eve had kept a candle burning in the front window of her Fourth Street home. It burned no more. The search for America's child had ended.

Seven

MOURNING POLLY

"I would rather have been putting my arms around her than putting my head on her casket."

She had spent two months alone, buried beneath plywood slabs, but Polly was alone no longer. After Davis had pointed to the dumping ground outside Cloverdale, FBI agents and county lawmen staked out the weed-strewn turf and set to the work of gathering not only Polly's remains, but the bits and pieces of evidence that would further tie Davis to the crime.

Outside the Petaluma Police Department, Chief Dennis DeWitt broke the horrible news to the media. A gasp rose from the crowd as reporters froze and lifted their pens for an instant. Behind the doors of the police station, officers wept. So many had spent so much time on the case; there was no way to suck it up and carry on without emotion.

"It affects us all greatly," DeWitt told the media. "When you help and care it takes a toll."

Reporter Randi Rossman was in the crowd listening to DeWitt's message that night.

"It was very somber," Rossman recalled. "It was the one time I did not get tipped off to the news in advance. As the reporters gathered before the press conference, we all thought Polly must be dead."

Still shaken from having broken the horrible news to Polly's family, Mershon and Parks dove north to check on the FBI men now sifting through what was left of Polly Klaas. From a distance the Cloverdale site looked like a movie set, as powerful lights lit up a swath of ground amid a blanket of darkness.

"It was the darkest night you could imagine," Mershon recalled. "But the light lit up the crime scene like the Las Vegas strip."

Police and FBI agents blocked off the Cloverdale site and placed a tarp over Polly's body to preserve the area that night. They set up tents to prevent the media from viewing their actions. The next morning they placed her remains on a red stretcher and carried them away. Mourners and reporters gathered across the road while fifty investigators, many wearing protective jumpsuits and masks, worked over the scene collecting evidence.

As the sun set, a federal investigator wept and placed two bunches of poinsettias on the ground where Polly was found. No one asked the agent to make the sweet gesture. He had kids of his own and was not the only federal man shaken by what had occurred. Another agent, who had seemed unaffected as he went about the task of gathering evidence at the site, broke down as he headed away from the crime scene.

"This is a guy who is tough as nails," an FBI spokesman said. "Driving home he started crying. He had trouble seeing down the road."

Across the county, volunteers at the Polly Klaas Center in Petaluma closed their door to the media and mourned privately. They put security men outside to keep reporters away. They didn't need cameras in their faces. Candles were lit everywhere.

"We had been taking leads right up until the end," said center volunteer Maureen Dixon. "We had hoped Davis had passed her off to someone. When the news came it was a big shock. I don't think we ever prepared ourselves. We did not want to believe anyone could do that to her."

Almost immediately the center started receiving calls about other missing children and changed its focus to become a beacon for other kidnap victims. Preston Bailey, Polly's music teacher, stayed all night and kept the place open in case anyone needed to sob with a companion. As dawn on Sunday approached, only Bailey and two other volunteers remained. They talked about locking the place up and going home, but Bailey didn't think that was wise. Outside stood a lone woman, staring at all the candles. Bailey greeted her.

"That is why we stayed through the morning. We could not leave her alone out there," he said.

Davis, meanwhile, had been transferred from the lock up in Mendocino County to the county jail at Santa Rosa. Mendocino County Sheriff's Sgt. Kevin Broin was happy to see the area's number one suspect out of his life. His office had been hearing about death threats made against Davis. There were plenty of people who wanted the man dead, Broin told the *Santa Rosa Press Democrat.* They packed him up and booked him into the Santa Rosa jail on suspicion of murder and kidnapping on Sunday and placed Davis on a suicide watch inside an isolation cell.

When the accused killer was brought before the court Tuesday morning he wore a bulletproof vest beneath his blue jailhouse jumpsuit. Eight uniformed deputies stood in the courtroom along with a number of plainclothes officers. Everyone attending was searched with a metal detector. The sixty-four-seat courtroom was packed. Forty people watched outside the courtroom doors on television monitors. They charged Davis with murder, kidnapping, two counts of assault with a deadly weapon, robbery, burglary, and two counts of false imprisonment. Prosecutors also alleged special circumstances that could bring a death sentence.

Prosecutors would later charge Davis with committing a lewd and lascivious act on a child under fourteen and intending to kill a victim while lying in wait.

"The only effect is it will make it more difficult to get a fair trial," Sonoma County Deputy Public Defender Barry Collins told the press. "My main concern is it is going to cause more public outrage."

"What we have here is a crime that impacted a family, a state and society," prosecutor Greg Jacobs said. "It is such an unnecessary senseless act. It destroyed the idea that a child is safe in a bedroom. We will never know the extent of the damage, the mental trauma he caused Polly Klaas. The idea of her suffering for at least anywhere from half an hour to hours, from being kidnapped, confined and tied and bound makes this case what it is."

The deck was being stacked against Davis whose court-appointed attorneys angled for a deal that would keep him out of the gas chamber. One of the lawyers, Sonoma County Public Defender Marteen Miller, told the press his client had confessed and was mystified the girl never screamed during the ordeal. Davis had stuck with the story about the beer and the drug-laced marijuana. He said he was under the influence of narcotics during the crime. Miller conceded the drug-induced haze was no excuse for murder, but hoped it might be enough to keep his client out of Death Row.

"I firmly believe that he is sincerely remorseful," Miller told the press. "He says he alone is responsible for this."

It is rare for a defense attorney to admit his client's guilt so soon after an arrest. Miller had hoped his honest assessment might pressure the District Attorney into a plea bargain that would keep Davis behind bars for life.

Miller, Sonoma County's Public Defender since 1965, said his actions were aimed at saving Davis's life. He said he didn't want to add hardship upon the Klaas family with a long public trial. He had hoped his appeal for a plea bargain would pressure the District Attorney to consider the public expense of a couple million dollars for the trial.

But Gene Tunney was not in a mood to bargain.

Tunney had been the top lawman in Sonoma County for twenty years and had been a leading campaigner against the California Supreme Court, which in the 1980s moved away from capital punishment. He had seen the faces of too many crime victims through the years and had developed his own system of seeking justice. For Tunney, some cases were too repugnant to let stand without balancing the scales.

Under Tunney's tenure only three other men convicted of murder received death sentences.

"Based on their crimes, they deserved the death penalty," Tunney told the *Press Democrat* in 1990. "The bottom line is that the death penalty is appropriate if limited to certain types of crimes. I never felt it immoral to put someone to death. There are certain people who are incapable of functioning in society without injuring everyone around them. I think the death penalty should not be applied lightly, but it should be applied to dangerous offenses and dangerous people."

There would be plenty of time to debate the merits of state execution as Davis's case slowly moved through the Sonoma County court system. For now it was time to mourn the death of a little girl who did a mean impression of Elvis. The pain of Polly's loss could not be measured. For two months America had read, seen and listened to news about her. She had become part of everyone's routine. Now the country had to deal with the loss.

"It feels like it was my kid out there," Eureka florist Paul Vegnani told the *San Jose*

Mercury News as he placed garlands at the Cloverdale site three days after Davis led officers to Polly's body. "I feel like I lost one of my own."

"I'm hearing from all kinds of people," San Jose-based psychiatric social worker Elinor Sheldon told the *Mercury News.* "It's the most widespread thing I've seen since the 1989 (Loma Prieta) earthquake."

Callers jammed the phone lines on radio talk shows. Strangers stopped by the Cloverdale site to leave messages, flowers, teddy bears, Christmas ornaments, and crosses. Schoolchildren lit candles and prayed, memorials were held, celebrities and political giants came to Petaluma to weep.

"This has really hit people," Bay Area radio call-in show host Ronn Owens told the *Mercury News.* He dedicated three hours of airtime to the story after Davis's confession. His phone lines were swamped.

"She was a young, sweet innocent victim," Kentucky sociologist Ronald Holmes told the *Mercury News.* "This kind of kidnapping reinforces for us that there are monsters out there and we can't protect ourselves no matter what we do."

The effort to find Polly Klaas had been the most extensive search for a kidnapped child in FBI history, bureau spokesman Rick Smith said. The FBI had assigned seventy-five agents, including a twenty-six-member evidence response team to the case. Thousands of volunteers had taken part in the search effort.

"Polly touched the deepest wellspring of human emotion, that place inside each of us where the love we feel for our own children resides," *Mercury News* columnist Jim Trotter wrote. "She touched both our love and our fear, and in doing so, she became our own. Her picture was everywhere. Her smile was imprinted in our conscious thought."

The thoughts poured out five days after Davis's confession when the country's mighty and small, the famous and the unknown gathered in Petaluma's St. Vincent de Paul Church, just blocks away from where Polly once posed like a lion on her porch. The stars wore black. Joan Baez sang "Amazing Grace," director George Lucas provided strobe lights, President Clinton sent a letter, California Gov. Pete Wilson talked tough on crime, U.S. Senator Dianne Feinstein was somber and Linda Ronstadt brought the house down as she sang "Somewhere Out There" while holding Annie Nichol's hand. The city's historic church played host to a grand event. Bay Area television stations canceled regular shows to broadcast the story live. The saddened masses lined up for the service hours before the church doors opened. Six hours before the service, the line stretched for several blocks.

A thousand made it inside. Nearly 500 stood outside in the rain and listened to the service on loudspeakers. Some silently held candles as rain drops bounced off umbrellas. Others were angry that politicians got in while they stood in the mist. Bill Rhodes, the man who helped fuel the search effort by turning his print shop into Polly Klaas central, watched the event on television.

"I'm grieving doubly," he told the Santa Rosa paper. "I'm grieving for Polly and for the loss of my activities at the foundation."

Inside, the spectacle moved all to tears. Michael Groves, a Klaas family friend, spoke to the crowd. Amid the weeping that rose from the pews, he told the audience that Polly had been on the edge of womanhood. She would have made a wonderful mother, he said.

"She was above all else an adoring and adored child. We love you Polly. We will always love you," Groves said.

Lavender ribbons decorated the pews. A picture of Polly in her favorite polka dot sweater stood amid a wreath of purple flowers. Eve Nichol sat next to Capt. Pat Parks. Sgt. Mike Meese read a poem Parks had written to honor the dead child.

"She was a compassionate and kind child who brightened the lives of everyone she knew," President Clinton wrote in a letter read at the ceremony by U.S. Representative Lynn Woolsey. "Her death is a terrible tragedy unbelievably difficult to accept. We must draw strength from the knowledge that so many people bound together to help Polly and her loved ones in her moment of need."

To Senator Feinstein, Polly was, "The symbol of every family's nightmare." Polly's story, Feinstein said, spoke of the world's brutality. At Petaluma Junior High School plans were already under way to remember the young girl with a memorial garden. Assistant Principal Joel Baum mentioned a need to remember her with something living. When his musing hit the press, volunteers sprouted everywhere. People donated plants, soil, stone and flowers. An artist supervised the project and helped students design a mural to accompany the field of childish dreams and the purple flowers that spelled out Polly's name.

"We wanted something that was joyful and celebrated youth and Polly's spirit," Baum said. "It is not a memorial of unhappiness and death, but a celebration of what Polly represented."

The school garden has since become a place of reflection for students. It stands near the front of the school, just off the parking lot. It sits away from the school's main courtyard. Students don't have to walk past the growing shrine unless they choose to. It is an inspirational spot. The flowers are no longer arranged to spell out Polly's name. Now they grow in random order in hues of purple and yellow to represent the school colors. Drawings of unicorns, the Cat in the Hat, hang gliders, and flowing streams serve as a backdrop. At one end rests a 450-pound basalt boulder engraved with Polly's name and the dates of her birth and death. Behind the rock is a drawing of piano keys, which carry upon the black and white stripes the words of a poem written by Polly's grandfather, Joe Klaas: "My Polly's face smiles out at me from every window that I see," it reads.

The colorful mural is filled with images of child fantasies. There are pink toadstools here, a smiling yellow star is dressed in blue-and-white striped overalls, a river flows through a stand of pine trees, and a girl with black hair rides a blue unicorn. A rainbow of hearts and flowers arcs over the green hills of Petaluma. A pot of gold waits at the rainbow's end. A blooming rose bursts with color on the mural wall, Polly's face emerges within its petals. A castle floats in clouds above the drawn land, and a lone candle burns bright in the window of a home.

"It is an uplifting and sacred place on campus," Baum said.

In Cloverdale, the townsfolk followed suit and created an unofficial memorial of wildflowers on the site where the girl fell.

Steve Connolly had taught music for forty-

four years in Cloverdale. He didn't know
Polly Klaas, but he knew hundreds of kids
just like her. He lives a quarter-mile from
the spot where Polly's body was found. He
is one of several Cloverdale residents who
tend the garden that mourners and volunteers planted in the girl's honor to transform
the ominous wood mill into a shrine.

"I've done it [the tending] ever since . . ."
Connolly said, unwilling to finish a sentence
that ended with a negative image. He comes
to the shrine every night to water the flowers, plant new ones and pick up fallen leaves.

"I don't know why," Connolly continued.
"She was a music girl, a band kid. For some
reason that focused on me and I thought of
all the kids I ever had in class."

Polly also calls to mind his three grown
daughters, and brings the seventy-five-year-
old man back to a time when they were small
and fragile.

"I taught band at Cloverdale High School
and taught the choir," he said. "I knew her
age group fairly well, so it really hit me. She
seemed like an outstanding kid."

When news of her death broke, Connolly
walked from this home to the fated spot. He
had walked across that path countless times
in his life. To him, the shrine is sacred. The
roadside attraction had started from that
spontaneous gesture of an FBI agent placing
poinsettias on the spot where they found

Polly. But weeks later it had become a re-pository of grief. Among the candles, flags, pieces of heart-shaped wood, and a tall wooden cross sat a basketball, left in tribute from a Mendocino College women's team.

But not everyone shared Connolly's affec-tion with the place, or wanted Polly remem-bered this way.

"My God, everyone in town has to drive by it every day and see it when they go," Cloverdale's vice Mayor Jim Teague told the *Press Democrat* one month after Polly's body was found on the community's doorstep. "We all respect Polly Klaas and it's very un-fortunate, but it's almost like the city of Cloverdale is being held hostage to some-thing that happened outside the city limits."

It was time to get on with the job of living, he said. His was not the only voice opposed to the growing shrine.

"That spot is dark and evil, despite all the flowers and the cross and the teddy bears," a Cloverdale resident told the press.

"It can't be stopped," another resident said. "What they are doing is making some-thing ugly, beautiful."

There was talk of turning the site into a park, but the Klaas family only wanted flow-ers to rest upon the spot their daughter was found.

"I don't want to memorialize the place where my little baby's body was found,"

Marc Klaas said. "Although I do feel it's a very powerful location."

By February, four months after Polly was abducted, her body was returned to her family. The final medical examinations had been completed. It was time for her to come home. Three dozen friends and relatives gathered in a small Petaluma chapel to spend a quiet moment around her closed casket. The six-hour visitation was nothing like the public memorial service held just two months before. There were no speeches or celebrities. It was just an opportunity for people to spend time with Polly. They cremated Polly and scattered her remains at sea near her grandparents' home in Carmel.

"We have been waiting to get her back for 123 days," Marc Klaas told the *Press Democrat*. "I would rather have been putting my arms around her than putting my head on her casket."

With Polly finally gone to rest, it was time to find out what went wrong and why a man like Davis was not only walking the streets free, but why he escaped detection for so long. The Petaluma cops reevaluated their procedures to be more responsive to the role the media could play in cases of this nature.

The Sonoma County Sheriff's Department investigated their missed opportunity in the case and the analysis led to reform. Sheriff Mark Ihde ordered that required information on major crimes be sent out on all department radios and that dispatchers doublecheck with any agency putting restrictions on all points bulletins. He also pledged to put computer terminals in every patrol car, allowing deputies immediate access to dispatch, vehicle and confidential information on suspects interviewed by officers.

The *Mercury News* reached a more damning conclusion in mid-December when its investigation determined the state's criminal justice system, which had failed to keep Davis behind bars, could not correctly track the accused child killer. Prison records led officials to conclude Davis was actually behind bars the night Polly was kidnapped, the *Mercury News* reported.

"Five months after he was paroled, the Department of Justice, the central repository for all criminal records in the state, still has Davis listed as being in prison," the newspaper reported. "Budget cuts could be cited as one factor. Since 1988, state officials have repeatedly turned down requests for a statewide database that would have flagged Davis as a parolee from another county."

The program would have cost $123,000, according to the *Mercury News*. Yet, Califor-

Polly Hannah Klaas in July, 1993, making costumes for a play. (*Scott Manchester/SYGMA*)

KIDNAPPED
AT KNIFE POINT

Polly Hannah Klass

D.O.B. 1/3/81
Brown Hair • Brown Eyes
4'10" – 80 lbs.

SUSPECT

White Male Adult 30-40 yrs.
Approx. 6'3" Dark/Dark Gray Hair
Full Beard, Wearing Dark Clothing
With Yellow Bandana Around Head

LAST SEEN OCTOBER 1, 1993 in PETALUMA, CALIF
If you have any information on this child
**CALL THE PETALUMA POLICE: 707-778-4481
or THE KEVIN COLLINS FOUNDATION: 800-272-0012**

Millions of these handbills were distributed to help
find Polly. (*AP/Wide World*)

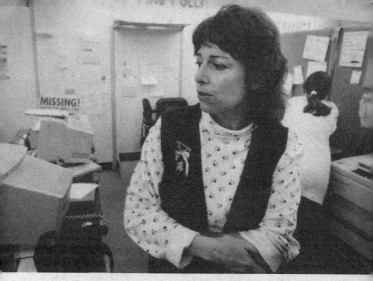

Eve Nichol, Polly's mother, at the Search
Command Center. (*AP/Wide World*)

Marc Klaas, Polly's father, spent countless days at the
Search Command Center, helping to search for his
missing daughter. (*AP/Wide World*)

One of the hundreds of volunteers working with the Search Command Center in downtown Petaluma, California, several days after Polly was abducted. (*AP/Wide World*)

Joe Klaas, Polly's grandfather, was a great source of comfort to his family and friends during the two-month ordeal before Polly was found. (*AP/Wide World*)

Volunteers at the Search Command Center in Petaluma watching news reports after suspect Richard Allen Davis was taken into custody. (*AP/Wide World*)

A police composite drawing of the
man who abducted Polly.
(*SYGMA*)

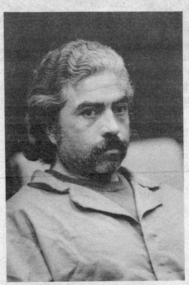

Richard Allen Davis, 39.
(*AP/Wide World*)

FOR A BRIEF
TIME AN
ANGEL RESTED
HERE.

The seven-foot-tall cross erected as a temporary memorial
on the site in Cloverdale, California, where Richard Allen
Davis led police to Polly's body. (*AP/Wide World*)

Signs expressed sympathy and remorse outside the office
of the Polly Klaas Foundation in Petaluma days after Polly's
body was found. (*AP/Wide World*)

Actress Winona Ryder, who had offered a $200,000 reward for Polly's safe return, being comforted by Joe Klaas at the Search Command Center after learning of Polly's death. (*Meri Simon*/Contra Costa Times, *1993*)

Winona Ryder places a teddy bear in memory of
Polly at the shrine outside the center.
(*Meri Simon*/Contra Costa Times, *1993*)

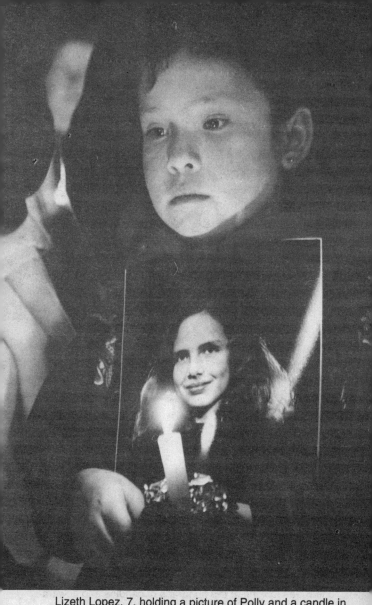

Lizeth Lopez, 7, holding a picture of Polly and a candle in her memory outside the volunteer center in Petaluma. (*AP/Wide World*)

Joe Klaas looking at the hundreds of candles and flowers
placed outside the Search Command Center.
(*AP/Wide World*)

B.J., Polly's grandmother, and Jonathan Klaas, Polly's uncle, at the Search Command Center after the discovery of Polly. (*AP/Wide World*)

U.S. Senator Dianne Feinstein comforts Marc Klaas just before Polly's memorial service. (*AP/Wide World*)

More than fifteen hundred people gathered at the St. Vincent de Paul Catholic Church where the memorial service for Polly was held. (*AP/Wide World*)

Eve Nichol surrounded by friends and family after the memorial service. (*AP/Wide World*)

Marc Klaas, with Vermont State Senator Susan Sweetser, left, and Gene Schmidt of Leewood, Kansas, testifies on Capitol Hill on March 1, 1994, during the House Crime and Criminal Justice Subcommittee concerning tougher legislation for three-time violent offenders.
(*AP/Wide World*)

Polly Hannah Klaas, her memory will live in the hearts
of everyone who fights to protect our children.
(*AP/Wide World*)

nia Attorney General Dan Lungren didn't fund the system. Instead, according to the newspaper, he bought new cars for his department. That analysis would be used against Lungren in the November 1994 election, by his Democratic challenger Tom Umberg. Joe Klaas joined the anti-Lungren team by filming a television commercial at his granddaughter's roadside shrine in Cloverdale. The ad showed Joe Klaas, dressed in a T-shirt that reads: "Remember Polly, Dump Lungren."

"I can't express the horror my family felt when we read in different newspapers that this registration and computer program was not operating and that it could have saved Polly's life," Joe Klaas later told the press when questioned why he made the ad.

Lungren said the budget cuts that gutted the computer system were forced by reductions brought on by the Democrat-controlled state legislature. He won reelection with ease.

When Davis was arrested in October 1993 for drunken driving, the offense violated his parole and would have sent him back to prison. Yet, Davis's parole officer did not find out about the arrest until November 29 when the FBI and Petaluma officers jailed Davis near his sister's home. The parole officer never knew, the *Mercury News* reported, because the Department of Corrections and the Department of Justice computers weren't designed to access each other's information easily. Parole officers rely on offenders to tell them about their law breaking.

Did the system fail Polly Klaas? Depends on who's talking.

"Every time there is a case where someone is on parole and commits a crime or kills someone, you hear that argument," prosecutor Jacobs said. "We don't have the time or resources [to make a perfect system]. We don't have a science fiction technology and can't rewire a criminal's brain."

Eight

THE BOY THEY
CALLED RICK

"He used to find stray dogs and cut them up."

Richard Allen Davis never had much of a chance. Born June 2, 1954, the third of five children, his parents split up when Davis was eleven. The kid neighbors called "Rick," turned sour early in life. He never really had a childhood or a real home. As a boy, Davis shuffled from place to place in San Francisco, Chowchilla and Fremont, living with his father, a grandparent and a series of stepmothers brought into his life following his folks' divorce. The closest thing to a stable existence came in La Honda, California, a hamlet of 580 people tucked beneath the heavy branches of thick trees midway between Redwood City and Half Moon Bay.

It's a stunning place. At night the sky is so clear you can track satellites with your eyes. Giant Santa Cruz Mountain redwoods sway in the wind, creaking like the well-worn floors of the town's only bar called Apple Jacks. People have tossed back shots inside the La Honda road house since 1920. The tavern has the feel of a place where people come to drink hard liquor and get drunk fast. The patrons, mostly locals who cut wood or build homes for a living, wear baseball caps and flannel shirts. Shiny amber glass ashtrays rest on dark wood tables scarred from years of use. The interior is lined with dirty work caps that hang like the heads of dead animals from the bar's wood walls. The juke box is vintage 1970. You can get six plays for a dollar.

The bar itself is cluttered with trinkets, including a wasp's nest that dangles from a string by the cash register. Bumper stickers plastered to the walls advise that the dive is "not responsible for women left overnight." Another reads: "The meek shall inherit shit."

In the mid '60s and early '70s, before Silicon Valley yuppies roosted amid the trees and turned up the heat on property values, La Honda was a rowdy town with three bars and plenty of biker types to add a little earthy charm. It was here, within earshot of thundering Harleys, beneath the giant trees of La Honda, where Rick Davis first tasted crime and felt a warm glow within his dark soul.

Before his parents divorced, Rick's mom, Evelyn McGuire, would bring her boyfriends to the family home, according to one court document. Young Rick didn't like that. The experience of seeing his mother entertain lovers in the family home caused Davis to harbor deep resentment, one psychiatrist later wrote.

"She was a very stern disciplinarian, on one occasion burning his [Rick's] hand for having smoked," noted Dr. Leonti H. Thompson, who provided a psychiatric review of Rick Davis in 1978. "After the divorce he went to live with his father and life was disturbed there as well."

Rick Davis moved about and had a hard time relating to each of the three women his father married. A dislike for all things female had been planted, according to the doctors who later probed Rick's mind. Court documents termed Rick Davis's nurturing years as emotionally deprived.

"Davis has had poor relationships with women throughout most of his life," Thompson wrote. "It is hard to determine the exact reason for this but [it] would appear that his early relationship with his mother may have set the stage for some of his later conflicts."

A loveless childhood may have also played a role, the experts concluded. They said he received few signs of affection during his formative years from his father and was almost entirely separated from his mother at an early age. Despite growing up within one of the most stunningly beautiful settings in

Northern California, the empty homelife left Davis with a terrible self-image, the doctors concluded. The child had turned into a living time bomb with an innate desire to hurt women.

By the time Rick reached junior high school, he had taken to stealing.

"Richard has suffered rejection by both parents as a child and no doubt bears considerable scarring from this," wrote Dr. George L. Ponomareff in an April 1977 psychiatric evaluation. "However, his pattern of taking goods, possibly to make up for the love and security that was not given to him, was well established by early adolescence."

With a reclusive father, who ran a tattered trailer park at the end of town, to guide him, Davis had little to look up to. He hung out with La Honda losers and got local drunks to buy his dead-end friends booze. The boys sipped themselves silly behind Apple Jacks near a bridge that spans La Honda Creek.

"There is no excuse for what he [Davis] has done, but he had no discipline as a child," said a La Honda resident who knew Davis.

By the time Rick Davis was twelve he had stolen checks from mailboxes, burglarized homes and forged documents. It might be easy to excuse the small crimes as the typical misdeeds of a confused boy. But something

different was at work here. These were not
the signs of adolescent growing pains, they
were hints of a disturbed person, mainly because Davis enjoyed them. The petty acts felt
good to the youngster. It was more than just
a thrill. The crimes left him with a "glow-
ing" feeling, according to one psychiatric
profile. The pattern developed over time.

Still, Davis proved popular enough to be
elected sergeant-at-arms in his sophomore
year at Pescadero High School, according to
the *San Francisco Chronicle*. Records show he
seldom attended class and accomplished little when he did show up. Davis tested low
in reading, spelling and math. With the ex-
ception of biology, driver's training and art,
his grades were below average or failing. He
dropped out of school in 1971.

"When he was not drinking he was not too
bad," a La Honda local said. "I remember
one time he went three weeks without drinking. Then he was a pretty decent guy. He
was halfway congenial. When Davis drank,
he looked pissed-off at the world. He was a
punk and he always got in trouble."

"He made a point of letting people know
that he carried a knife, and he used to find
stray dogs and cut them up," a former La
Honda resident remembered. "Everyone
feared him. He was just terribly intimidating.
You'd look at him and those eyes would
speak to you— evil."

It was said by former neighbors that as a child Rick Davis doused cats with gasoline and watched them burn. Another story has him taking down a cow, then chopping the animal up for its meat. Napa psychiatrist Dr. Llewellyn M. Jones examined Davis in March 1978. He said Davis exhibited sadistic traits.

Despite a past riddled with abuse and destruction, some found glimmers of hope in young Rick.

"He was a quiet, loner kid," Pescadero High School soccer coach Jim Crawley told the *San Francisco Chronicle*. "I had no problems with him. He didn't seem to have problems with other kids."

Rick's sister, Darlene Schwarm remembers his kind side.

"Rick brought me up, he raised me," said Darlene, who was two when her parents divorced. "When I came home from school he would be there. When I got up in the morning he would be there. He cooked and cleaned. He was my father and my mother."

The kidnapping and murder have taken their toll on the Schwarms. Not only were they ostracized by their community in Ukiah, but they faced drug charges in connection with small amounts of methamphetamine authorities found on their property while they searched for Davis. The Schwarms are not sophisticated people. They fit the definition of the Apple Jacks bumper sticker about meek people inheriting very little. They can't fight off the forces that have come against them, thanks to Rick. Still, Dick and Darlene Schwarm can't fully accept that Davis may have murdered a young girl. Darlene still questions the murder charges. She clings to the hope that perhaps others were involved and that maybe her brother is just the fall guy—a career con too proud to break the criminal's code of honor and rat out the real murderer.

Dick Schwarm is equally confused by it all. He claims to have some understanding of his brother-in-law. He can't see how any man who had committed so horrible a crime could keep it to himself.

"I don't know at this point in time," Dick Schwarm said nearly a year after the crime. "I have some things I have to figure out. I am trying to put the whole puzzle together from my experiences with him. We have never had problems with him; never got in no trouble with me. I can't see him sitting around the house with our girls and have neighbors' girls come and round and not have any remorse about it."

The Schwarms' attorney, Erik R. Petersen ties it all back to the La Honda days, where life turned rough.

"To see him and talk to him it is amazing to think he could commit a crime like this," Petersen said. "But then no one suspected

Ted Bundy was killing people either. He seems like a normal uneducated guy."

Darlene Schwarm remembers there was little closeness among her clan, but said her father was not the boozing thug others remember. She said he was never drunk around her and never abusive to her in any way. But Robert Davis was tough on Rick.

"I would get my brothers in trouble sometimes," Darlene Schwarm said. "It was penny-ante stuff. One time Rick got his jaw broke [by their father]."

Darlene Schwarm chuckled at the memory of her father's outburst, but could not remember what she did to set the violence in motion. Darlene Schwarm is equally blank about her mother.

"I could not even tell you what her favorite color was or nothing," she said.

But La Honda residents remember Rick Davis well enough and the community sighed with relief in 1971 when a judge offered him the option of doing time in a camp for juvenile delinquents or joining the Army. The Army took him at seventeen. The military life didn't change Davis. The Army discharged him after thirteen months because of fights, arguments, and an inability to adjust to military discipline.

"I didn't want to go in," Davis told a court-appointed psychiatrist in 1978. "They said I wasn't ready for the Army."

Davis, who never seemed without a handy excuse to pin his troubles upon, blamed his problems on drugs and alcohol. After one military binge, Davis learned he had pulled a knife and cut someone while in the service in Germany, Dr. Thompson stated in his 1978 psychiatric report. The person he had cut had merely offered to shake his hand. On another occasion, Davis stole liquor, got drunk and tore up a girlfriend's house. The military discharged him in August 1972.

"I had to go in the Army," Davis said during a 1990 tape-recorded prison conversation with a Santa Clara County prosecutor. "It was '71, they shipped me to Germany. I left here and hash was four dollars a gram. I get to Germany and it's sixty cents a gram. So I go wild. I start getting loaded like a motherfucker, hash, coke, opium and shooting morphine. Then I got kicked out."

Next came a series of low-end jobs ranging from a utility man in Menlo Park where he earned $2.50 an hour, to a gas station attendant in San Mateo in 1973. He was fired by the gas station owner in May 1973 after being arrested for a traffic warrant charge. After that he got by cutting and selling wood. His return to La Honda only brought more bad news. In 1973, his former girlfriend, Marlene Voris, committed suicide just days after she received a commission in the Navy. Voris celebrated the good news about her

Navy assignment by partying with friends, according to an account in *The New Yorker.*

"At the end of the party, everyone left together, but Rick said he had to go back," Ruth Baron, a La Honda resident, told the magazine. "He went back to the house and a few minutes later there was a gunshot."

Handwritten notes were found and authorities quickly wrote the death off as self-inflicted. After Davis's role in the Polly Klaas investigation emerged, authorities reopened the Voris case. Once again, the San Mateo County Sheriff's Department ruled the matter a suicide. Investigators reexamined seven handwritten suicide notes Voris left in 1973. They concluded that the eighteen-year-old woman drank with Davis and other friends in her parents' living room and played with a rifle. Voris died from a shot to the head.

Davis would later tell Dr. Ponomareff that Voris killed herself "almost in his presence." Ever since her death, Davis claimed to hear her voice telling him things, usually of a comforting nature. On other occasions, the voice told him to do bad things.

From February to August 1973, Davis was arrested for public drunkenness, resisting arrest, burglary, contributing to the delinquency of a minor, and drug charges. Once, after being arrested for drunkenness, Davis lashed out at Redwood City police officers. They had found him lying against the pas-

senger's window of his car, he turned bellig-
erent and tried striking them with his feet.
After they cuffed him and put him in a patrol car, Davis kicked at the windows. They
fined him $25.

Redwood City officers found him drunk
again in August, leaning against some
hedges. He had urinated in his pants and
could not walk without their help. Davis
broke into a retreat cabin in La Honda in
October, slept in the bed, drank all the
owner's alcohol and walked off with $751 in
various items. He later admitted burglarizing
two other cabins. In all, Davis had walked
away with a camera, a leather jacket and
tools. Some of the goods were found at San
Francisco pawn shops. He blamed the burglary spree on hunger and alcohol.

"Early that day I was over in Redwood City
at this party drinking," Davis said at the
time. "I do not remember when I got home
but there was only some potatoes there so I
took a walk up into La Honda to see my
friend's house but no one was there."

Spotting an empty cabin, Davis broke in.

"I knew it was just a place where the people come to on the weekends, so I went up
there to see if I could find the key."

He stumbled and fell into a window shat-
tering the glass.

"Since it was broken I went through it to
see if I could find some food," he said.

Davis confessed, saying: "I knew what I did was wrong, so I figured I should get punished for it."

By December 1973, the good people of La Honda had grown so sick of Davis, there was talk he might not survive an extended stay in his adopted home town.

"The citizens of La Honda are very upset over the defendant and his involvement in numerous residential burglaries and thefts in their area," according to a probation report written after Davis pleaded guilty to a burglary charge. "If the defendant returns to that area his life may be in jeopardy. During this period of incarcerations he can attempt to complete his education and demonstrate that he is in fact interested in rehabilitating himself."

One of the officers who investigated the burglaries warned the court that Davis was a dangerous person who had no remorse. But Davis received a suspended sentence and probation, not prison. Davis left behind a pregnant girlfriend in La Honda. He had hoped they would end up together after his current troubles were cleared up.

"She indicated that the defendant was in need of psychiatric care," according to a 1973 probation report on Davis. "It appears that the defendant is more optimistic about their relationship than she is."

She gave birth to a son in 1974, but Davis

never helped support the boy, or seemed to care about the child, according to court records. He was arrested again December 5, 1973 for burglary and given a six-month sentence in San Mateo County. During his probation, the legal system did all it could to help. Court records indicate he received intensive supervision, welfare assistance, counseling on how to manage his money and advice on job opportunities. Nothing worked, and by May 13, 1974, Davis was in trouble again after being caught red-handed breaking into the South San Francisco High School. Davis again blamed his actions on hunger even though he had received a $100 welfare check ten days earlier.

"I had already spent the money and was hungry and had my mind on other things," Davis told his probation officer. "I seen [sic] the school and thought there would be a frigerator [sic] in the teacher's area, or else find the keys to the cafeteria."

He tripped an alarm while prowling. A police dog called to the scene sniffed him out. Davis wanted to be placed on work furlough after his conviction, because he could not "get loaded" in jail. He told officials that life behind bars was boring because he did not have enough room to walk around. By now, even Rick's dad, who was also helping him financially, had had enough of his incorrigible offspring.

"The investigating and arresting officer in this case concurs in the impression that the defendant does not seem concerned with avoiding jail," wrote Davis's probation officer David J. Mandel in the June 1974 court report. "The defendant needs to serve some time in the hope that he will tire of prison walls."

But Davis did not stay behind bars for long.

"Mr. Davis lacks both the courage and motivation to change his patterns," Mandel wrote at the time. "There is no question that he will be in State Prison within a few years, unless the Criminal Justice System is able to make a more profound impression on the defendant than has been the case so far."

Davis was in and out of jail and prison from March 1975 to April 1975 for grand theft, burglary, probation violations and jail escape. Along the way he cheated three fellow inmates on a drug deal and got shot. According to published reports, Davis absconded after getting a leave from the San Mateo County Jail. The three inmates had asked him to smuggle drugs into the jail, but Davis took off instead. After being released from the jail, the thugs caught up with Davis one day in March of 1975. They pistol-whipped him and forced him into a car. Davis escaped and was shot in the back. The three left him for dead.

The bullet passed cleanly through his back

and exited his chest. A passerby took Davis to a hospital where he recovered. But he still didn't learn and continued to take chances by breaking the law. From February 12, 1973 through August 2, 1976, authorities across the Bay Area arrested Davis twenty times.

Though Davis had been a prolific thief during his La Honda years, his crimes remained relatively harmless. All that was about to change.

Nine

VIOLENT CRIMINAL

"He lacks conscience and has no feeling of guilt or remorse."

Less than two months after his release from state prison on a burglary charge, Richard Davis was ready to graduate from the world of small-time theft to the realm of violent crime. He made his mark in dramatic fashion and terrorized three women from September 24 to December 20, 1976.

Davis had recently been paroled from prison and released in the Bay Area. He spotted a twenty-six-year-old legal secretary named Frances Mays as she walked to her blue Volkswagen parked near a Bay Area Transit Station in Hayward, California. Davis later told a court-appointed psychiatrist that he "heard" the voice of his dead girlfriend, Marlene Voris, telling him that the woman was asking for it. The voice told him she wanted to be raped. It was about 6:30 P.M.

Mays checked around before getting to her car. She had been cautious and wanted to make sure no one was following her. But Davis had a way of avoiding the human eye.

He appeared just as she opened the car door. In one hand he carried a knife. In the other he held a paper bag that contained rope.

"There was someone behind me and he said: 'I've got a knife at your back,'" Mays told the television news show "PrimeTime Live" in January 1994.

Davis ordered her into the car and told her to slide over to the passenger's side. He told her to take her shoes off. Mays, seeing the five-inch kitchen knife, offered the man her wallet. She set it on the seat and hoped that was all he wanted. She began to cry hysterically. He told her to shut up, then he hit her to emphasize the point. Davis explained that he was being followed and needed help to get out of town. Mays gave him her car keys and he told her to crouch down in the seat.

Davis next demanded she explain how to get out of the BART station so they would not be seen by too many people. He drove for about fifteen to twenty minutes. Along the way, Mays looked out of the window and made small talk with her abductor. She learned he had just gotten out of prison. He told her this kind of crime was not his normal game, before he pulled into a deserted area near a cement company five miles away from the station.

Mays may still have held out hope that Davis meant to use her to escape some unseen threat. After stopping the car he broke the news. No one was after him, he told her. No, this was Davis's game all along and this time he was the one doing the chasing. He was after her. He admitted that the ruse came in handy and kept her off guard. Davis liked to keep his victims confused.

He showed her the knife and began to unzip his pants.

"You know what I want you to do," he said.

He told Mays to treat him right or he would stab her, the frightened woman wrote in a police report. Davis pulled his right arm around Mays's head and shoulder. He began to pull her toward his crotch. He started to count to three.

At that very moment, off-duty California Highway Patrol Officer Harold James Wentz was heading to work with his wife, LaVonne.

Mays saw the approaching CHP car and began to scream. She tried to signal for help by hitting the horn to her car. Nothing came out because the engine had been turned off. She struggled with Davis and grabbed for the knife. It cut her left hand but distracted Davis enough so she could race free. She grabbed for the door and ran out into the parking lot.

LaVonne Wentz spotted the desperate-looking young woman in a red dress and beige coat standing in the road, waving her arms and shouting. Her husband got out and dashed to Mays, who pointed to the man now running in the distance.

"Stop him! He robbed me and tried to rape me!" Mays yelled.

LaVonne Wentz put Mays in the patrol car and tried to settle her down. She recalled that Mays had a small cut on her hand.

"She was hysterical," LaVonne Wentz said. "She kept reporting that he tried to hurt her and rape her."

Officer Wentz ran after Davis. He reached for his gun and leveled his service revolver at the man.

"I ordered him to halt," Officer Wentz reported after the crime. "He stopped, looked at me and started to run. I again ordered him to halt and raise his hands, which he did."

Davis knew the routine all too well. He did as the cop told him, just as he had done many times before. Davis walked backwards toward Wentz and laid face down on the ground.

Seven weeks of freedom were over. Davis's wrists again felt the cold embrace of steel handcuffs.

The horrifying half-hour ordeal altered Mays forever.

"I'm too extreme in my fear," Mays told the *San Jose Mercury News*. "I think I get panic attacks when people approach me in a parking lot. If I'm home I sleep with the lights on. If I'm alone, I check and check and double-check all the locks. I don't go anywhere alone."

Mays, who lives in Modesto, California with her husband and son, is expected to testify against Davis at his trial in connection with the Polly Klaas murder.

"I think I am lucky to be alive," Mays told the *Mercury News*. "I feel really bad for the Klaas family. Poor girl. Polly was only 12. If she went through everything I went through, it must have been terrifying."

While awaiting trial in Alameda County on charges of kidnapping and assault to commit rape, Davis tied a sheet around his neck and jumped off a jail cell toilet. A court psychiatrist interviewed Davis about the suicide try. He claimed that the voice of the long-dead Voris had guided his actions once again. He said he heard her sweet voice, thought about the good times they once had and stepped off the toilet bound for oblivion.

"The suicide attempt was associated with memories of a girlfriend's suicide," psychiatrist Joseph C. Davis reported after interviewing the suspect in April 1977.

On December 8, 1976, jail authorities moved him to Napa State Hospital for evaluation following the suicide try. Under loose hospital security, Davis walked away about one week later taking a sock filled with soap bars as a weapon. The town of Napa was in for a four-day crime wave. The next person to feel Davis's wrath was Marjorie Arlington, then a thirty-two-year-old registered nurse.

"I remembered being awakened by my head hurting," Arlington told a judge during a preliminary hearing against Davis in February 1978. "I was trying to figure out why it was hurting. I turned around and saw a man standing over me, hitting with an object."

The man was Davis. The object was a black steel fireplace poker. He hit her five times before Arlington chased him from her home. Davis later told psychiatrist Leonti H. Thompson that "voices" forced his hand. He said he impulsively attacked Arlington because he wanted to "relieve tension."

"He states that he had been responding to daydreams in which he heard a lady voicing her concern at what it was like to be beaten," Thompson wrote in his 1978 review of Davis's mental state.

Davis later told Dr. Ponomareff that Arlington secretly wanted punishment. "We both got something out of it," he told the psychiatrist.

After beating the woman, Davis plotted his next move. He hid out in a boat to avoid police after attacking the nurse, then searched for another victim. He awoke the next morning to the sounds of a couple's conversation inside a nearby home. He planned to wait until the man of the house left so he could steal some clothing. Davis next crept into the family's garage, armed himself with a saw and turned off the electricity hoping that the wife would come out to investigate. Luckily, the woman never showed. Instead, she called a neighbor and Davis fled seeking other targets.

On December 20, 1976, three days after the Arlington attack, he broke into a county animal shelter and stole firearms and animal tranquilizers. He walked away with a shotgun and ammunition.

Hazel Ellis became the next woman to face Davis. Ellis had just left a Napa tavern and walked toward her convertible at about midnight on December 20, when Davis spotted her. Ellis was alone, so Davis figured she wanted some "fun." Once again, he seemed to emerge from nowhere and take his victim by surprise.

"I opened my side of the door and a gentleman opened the other side of the door and got into the car with me," Ellis testified during a 1978 court hearing. "He had a shotgun which he put to my neck. He said he had to get out of town and that I was going to drive him."

Ellis had been drinking that night and told the armed abductor that he should drive. The bluff did not work. Davis got real serious and jammed the weapon farther into her throat. After a few minutes, Davis pulled some gauze

from his pocket. Ellis reasoned that her worst
nightmare had come to life.

"Well, I figured I had had it," Ellis said.

What Davis did not know was Ellis carried
a gun. She reached for a loaded .22 caliber
pistol she kept under her car seat.

"I decided to try to get out of my car,"
she said. "I slipped open my car door and
the interior light came on. I grabbed the pistol and rolled out of my car."

Davis made a break, too, as Ellis fired
three shots into the night. Although Ellis
had fairly good aim, Davis avoided death, or
serious injury, once again. Ellis next traveled
to a second bar and had a few drinks. She
shared her daring story with the bar-stool
gang, but was reluctant to report the inci-
dent to police because she did not have a
permit for the weapon. Her ex-husband per-
suaded her to call the cops, who wrote down
her story.

Davis capped his spree by returning to La
Honda where he broke into the house of
Josephine Kreiger. When she arrived home
December 21, 1976 she found cigarette butts
on the floor and opened Christmas gifts
tossed aside. Clothing, a sleeping bag and
twelve silver dollars were gone. Investigating
officers found Davis hiding out crouched in
a ball near a fence line. The shotgun, which
he had previously stolen from the Napa animal shelter, lay under his body.

"I drew my service revolver and told him to freeze," San Mateo County Sheriff's Deputy Guy Offsman said during a court hearing in January 1977.

Davis pleaded not guilty by reason of insanity to the charges, which brought an examination by doctors Thompson, Jones, Davis and Ponomareff. All found him sane, but clearly dangerous. Llewellyn M. Jones concluded that Davis's boyhood dream was to become a truck driver and that Davis enjoyed books like *The Executioner, The Butcher, Death Wish,* and *In Cold Blood.* Jones's March 13, 1978 report included the following information about Richard Davis:

"He masturbates two times daily and thinks of female victims of past crimes, tying them up and sodomizing them. He is a self-centered person with no regard for the rights or feelings of others, no close friends. He displays outbursts or tense, inappropriate laughter. He shows signs of latent homosexuality. He rationalizes his crimes by saying that the victims secretly desire to be robbed and assaulted, and, in a sense, are asking for it. He lacks conscience and has no feelings of guilt or remorse or regret over what he has done. His judgment is poor, impulse control poor, insight lacking. He does not think there is anything wrong with him."

Jones labeled Davis an antisocial psychopath, but determined Davis knew the crimes he committed were wrong and against the law.

"He harbors a great deal of hatred and hostility against women, who represent mother figures to him," Jones wrote. "He hates them because he feels that his mother did not give him love as a child. If released, he would be certain to resume his pattern of criminal behavior: theft, burglary and assaults against women. Because of these assaultive tendencies, he is considered to be extremely dangerous to others, especially women."

Jones ruled Davis legally sane. Dr. George L. Ponomareff did the same.

"He presents as an amiable, well spoken man who displays no evidence of disordered thought processes," Ponomareff wrote in April 1977. "He denies any delusions or hearing voices talking about him. The only abnormal content noted was that of the voices asking for violence to be done to them. We discussed the legality of his particular operations and he blandly insisted that while such behavior might be illegal under some circumstances, it was not in his case. I must admit that there is a possibility that he suffers from an encapsulated paranoid state with the hallucinations truly representing an uncontrollable impetus to violence, but I consider this very unlikely. The balance of the evidence from both history and examination suggests a basic diagnosis of sociopathic personality."

Dr. Joseph Davis reached a similar conclusion.

"Mental examination revealed an alert man who was garrulous," Davis wrote in his 1977 report. "His main thought content centered around explanation for his criminal behavior on the basis of recurrent obsessions and beliefs that he understands what people want him to do and then he proceeds to do . . . It is my conclusion that this man by history does have obsessions. There is a question about whether he was overtly psychotic at the time for the behaviors are well-organized and he describes himself as having had a 'restless urge.' These urges seem more obsessive than truly delusional; also, at the time of the commission of the offense, he was aware the act was wrong."

Thompson reported his findings in March 1978.

"Psychiatric evaluation revealed a muscular, dark-haired, alert young man who showed nothing bizarre or unusual during the interview," Thompson wrote. "He was friendly, cooperative and very much at ease. Speech was entirely logical, coherent. His emotional reaction appeared to be one of normal spontaneity with no significant anxiety or depression seen. His thought processes appeared to be entirely reality oriented. I detected no evidence of any delusions, fragmentation of thinking, scattering of thought. He did seem to show a rather manipulative type of thinking in which he phrased his version of events to produce the desired end result.

"Mr. Davis appears to have very little understanding of his inner psychological functioning and how he has managed to get into difficulties throughout his life. He seems to utilize massive denial in dealing with this aspect of his life. His judgment appears to be relatively intact for functioning in a structured environment. His judgment in the community appears to be poor and he appears to be at the mercy of underlying impulses. The basic impression that I gained of Mr. Davis is that he represents an antisocial reaction, severe, as manifested by a longstanding history of impulsive disorders, predatory behavior unmodified by punishment or learning, a shallow hedonistic view of life in which pleasures of the moment are seized without regard for the rights or needs of others. He has a life-long pattern of acting out behavior of a criminal or near criminal type. It is my feeling that the defendant did, in fact, know and appreciate the wrongfulness of his acts on December 17 and 20, 1976. . . . All of Mr. Davis's actions appear to have resulted from his underlying antisocial personality. It must be noted that individuals with this degree of character immaturity may frequently appear psychotic if they are observed over the short period. Such individuals are very adept at picking up clues as to behavior which will get them into a hospital setting in lieu of jail. I do not believe that Mr. Davis will profit from treatment in any mental health facility."

The doctors had spoken. Davis withdrew his insanity plea and took a plea bargain on the various charges. He received a sentence of one to twenty-five years for the Mays kidnapping. In exchange, prosecutors dropped the sex charge. He also got two years to life for the Napa assaults and six months to ten years for the La Honda burglary. Former Napa County District Attorney James Boitano, who negotiated a plea bargain with Davis, explained his logic to reporter Sam Donaldson on "PrimeTime Live."

"You can't [try every case]. You don't have the manpower," he said during the January 27, 1994 broadcast. "You don't have the deputies, you don't have the police, you don't have the judges and it is getting worse."

Before being sent to state prison in July 1977, Davis told a sentencing judge that his crimes didn't bother him.

"The probation report says that you expressed no remorse and that you consider the activity all right. Do you believe that?"

San Mateo Superior Court Judge Alan W. Haverty asked.

"If I felt bad about it, I wouldn't have done it," Davis replied.

"It doesn't bother you at all?" the judge asked.

"If it did I wouldn't have done it," Davis said.

"Well, that's your problem, Mr. Davis," the judge continued. "It ought to bother you."

Though on paper it appeared society might never have to worry about Davis ever again, a new California law then taking effect eliminated open-ended sentences. Davis's sentence of one to twenty-five years was recalibrated. Parole boards rejected his bid for early release six times, but under the new guidelines, he could serve no more than six years. By March 1982 he was loose again.

Soon after Davis was released from prison in 1982, he met Sue Edwards, a woman who would become his soulmate and partner in crime.

Sue was sixteen when she married Bill Edwards, a thirty-year-old auto parts dealer in Modesto, California. They ran off to Reno, Nevada for the ceremony in the Sierra Inn Wedding Chapel. They had two sons together.

Problems arose in the marriage. Accused of

molesting the boys, Bill was investigated but never charged. Sue ran off, leaving the children with their father. In 1982, she moved to Sunnyvale, California and ran with a fast crowd. She met Richard Allen Davis at St. James Infirmary, a popular mountain view bar there. According to a 1990 taped interview by Santa Clara Deputy District Attorney Lane Liroff with Davis, the people Sue knew there were causing her difficulties. Davis became her brave knight and rescued her.

"She didn't want to be involved with them, so I had to step in," Davis said. "They kind of backed off."

Bonded by a mutual taste for freedom and danger, Davis and Edwards hit the road. On November 30, 1984, they barged in on Selma Varich, a friend of Sue's sister. Varich was getting ready to leave her apartment in Redwood City when Davis and Edwards appeared.

"They started saying things to me," Varich told a San Mateo County judge in 1985. "The male had a handgun. The lady pulled the phone out of my wall. Just yanked it out of the wall. He kept saying me to 'shut up' and finally I got hit on the head with the gun," Varich said. "The guy was, you know, so elated with the fact that he was victimizing me that he— he was laughing and he was smiling," Varich told ABC's "PrimeTime Live."

Davis and Sue wanted money. They knew
Varich had a bank account. They ordered
her to withdraw her cash, otherwise, they
warned, the mob would wipe out her family.

"They said: 'There is a contract out on
you, your daughter and your father with the
mafia,' " Varich told the court.

She went to an American Savings branch
and withdrew $6,000. Sue, armed with a gun
Davis had given her, went with the terrified
Varich. Davis picked Sue up after she got
the money and the two fled town. Flush with
the stolen cash, but in danger of easy arrest
after preying on someone they knew, Davis
and Sue headed for fresh hunting grounds
in Kennewick, Washington.

They stayed one step ahead of the authorities until March 21, 1985 when the police in
Modesto, California pulled them over for a
broken taillight. Davis had warned Sue to get
rid of all her identification just in case the
cops ever stopped them. He had planned to
tell police that hitchhikers had ripped them
off and left them without wallets or any ID
cards. But when the officers found Sue's Social Security card, the game was over.

They were prosecuted for the Varich kidnapping and robbery. Davis, who had wooed
Edwards by acting as her brave knight years
before, played the role again and took pri-
mary responsibility for the crimes. He received sixteen years in prison. Sue Edwards

got a short jail term and probation. However, under the sentencing laws he was able to gain good-time credit and a release date of 1993. Edwards walked free after serving only six months in jail.

In 1988, Sue married Mike Mrava, an alcoholic engineer and settled down in Sunnyvale. On November 10 of the same year, Mrava was brutally murdered by Floyd Dwayne Bailey, an ex-con and friend of Sue Edwards.

But when Sue attempted to file a claim on Mrava's estate in Santa Clara County, she realized that she had never obtained an official divorce from her first husband. Hoping to rectify her oversight, she proceeded to file for divorce from Bill Edwards in another county.

Deputy District Attorney Lane Liroff, the man who got Bailey convicted of Mrava's murder, discovered Sue's mistake and subsequently prosecuted her for bigamy in May 1991. One of his star witnesses was Richard Allen Davis.

Called as a character witness at the bigamy trial while still serving his sentence, Davis demurred on the stand, fearing the jailhouse justice of his fellow inmates for helping law enforcement. According to Liroff, Davis may have clinched his case simply by entering the court in shackles, his tattoos prominently displayed by his short-sleeve prison uniform.

"He has almost a Cro-Magnon look . . . a presence of a very dangerous person," Liroff recalls. "He's big, strong and unkempt. He has a mountain look about him. There is an absolute cold sense of a killer. Everyone in the case knew that."

Showing casual photos of Davis and Edwards during her visits to him in prison seemed to leave the impression that anyone involved with him could not be totally innocent. Edwards was convicted and sentenced to six years in the Central California's Women's Facility in Chowchilla. She was released in the summer of 1994.

When Liroff prosecuted Bailey for Mrava's murder in 1993, Davis's name came up during a break. Liroff calculated that Davis would be a free man in the summer of that year. He remembers commenting on how dangerous he was.

Five months after this conversation, Davis was arrested in connection with the abduction and murder of Polly Hannah Klaas. "I really was not surprised," Liroff later commented to the press.

Ten

THE PROSECUTION

"Davis is the kind of guy who lives outside the normal conventions and rules of society. He is dangerous."

Greg Jacobs, the forty-six-year-old Sonoma County prosecutor spent his youth in Northern California's post-war boom and saw his hometown of Sebastopol shift from a farming center into a bedroom community for Bay Area yuppies.

"We have five coffee shops now," Jacobs said of the Russian River community of 7,000.

Like most attorneys, Jacobs could play either side of the criminal debate. He started out working for a defense attorney after law school but took a job with the Sonoma County District Attorney's Office to get trial experience. Time went on, he moved up the ladder. He's done twenty years.

"When I started in the job I did not know 99 percent of the defendants were guilty," Jacobs said.

As a young prosecutor in the early 1970s, Jacobs had trouble fitting in with the other deputy district attorneys stuck in their good-old-boy ways. They confused his affable manner and boyish smile for liberalism. He also didn't join the poker games with the office boys.

"I had problems in the office at first," Jacobs said. "I think the older guys thought I was too liberal because of my personality and because I swam instead of playing cards with them."

His small office inside a sprawling county government center in Santa Rosa is cluttered with detective stories, law books and stacks of legal papers. A tattered brown briefcase is on the floor. It is bursting at the seams. The office walls are decorated with paintings his mother made, and with bits of fishing mementos. His father's office sign hangs on a wall above his desk. John M. Jacobs was a longtime Sonoma County dentist. He committed suicide in 1986 when cancer got the best of him.

"It was terminal," Greg Jacobs said. "They could not treat him anymore. He went home and shot himself with his deer rifle."

Jacobs pondered a career change after his father's suicide and applied for a judicial post. But Republican George Deukmejian was in the governor's house in those years, and Jacobs, a registered Democrat, didn't have much of a chance. The post went to a Republican and Jacobs remained a prosecutor. Within a year he was made chief deputy.

Through twenty years, Jacobs had worked over one hundred trials and prosecuted a handful of murder cases. In recent years he has been more of an administrator.

The Klaas case is the most important of his career.

"The facts of the crime are extraordinary," Jacobs said. "You have the whole enchilada. You have Davis's background, the fact he eluded his just rewards earlier (on Pythian Road), the fact it happened in a small town. The police being accused of negligence. The fact that the guy led authorities to the body."

Jacobs had the flu the day investigators linked Davis to the crime.

"Mike Meese filled me in on the facts after I went home sick," Jacobs said. "He said there was going to be a briefing the next day. I told him I felt terrible and asked if I should come to the briefing. He said I better."

When Jacobs arrived at the Petaluma Police Station, FBI big shots were everywhere. The experts from Virginia had just matched the cloth found on Pythian Road with the straps used to bind Kate and Gillian. The case had come together and the lawmen were arranging arrest plans for Davis.

"I was being carried by the events," Jacobs said. "I was asked if they could proceed with the arrest even though they did not have a body. We had a lot of physical evidence to tie him to the kidnapping at that point. The question was, could we charge him with murder?"

Davis answered that question when he confessed and led Meese to Polly's body.

"After I got over the flu, I looked at myself in the mirror and felt the weight of the case," Jacobs said.

Jacobs is not the type to get emotionally involved in cases. He learned long ago that overzealous prosecution leads to mistakes and a short career.

"You have to stay pretty flat [emotionally]," he said. "Otherwise, you burn out and miss things. Other lawyers get too worked up over a case and they get sloppy. The jury looks at them and figures the lawyer is too emotional, is pushing too hard. People act negatively to unreasonable authority.

"The worst thing a district attorney can do is to forget he is a trial attorney first," Jacobs said. "A jury goes with the person who has presented himself in an honest effort. If I have my case [together] and an honest jury, I don't have to act. Becoming extremely emotional usually does not work.

"The toughest part is that my daughter probably knew who Polly was because they went to the same elementary school," Jacobs said. "Polly lived outside of town then and she was two years behind my youngest daughter, but I think they rode the bus together and they shared some of the same teachers."

Jacobs has not worked on a murder trial since 1986 when Thomas Allen Davies got a sentence of twenty-five-years to life for killing a twenty-year-old friend. The sentencing judge called the case, "one of the most vicious and needless crimes [he] ever presided over."

Davies, seventeen at the time, lured Richard Meier to an isolated spot in Mendocino County to raid a suspected marijuana garden. There was no weed, only a loaded gun at the end of the road.

"Davies set the man up," Jacobs said. "The victim was a happy-go-lucky guy who had a nice four-by-four truck and some money. Davies talked him into stealing marijuana and told him to bring $500 along to bribe a guard at the [at the marijuana patch]."

Davies shot his victim in the back. He and co-defendant, Peter Taneyhill, hauled Meier's body back to Santa Rosa and dumped it near the county government center. They drove Meier's pickup truck to Washington State. Taneyhill testified against Davies and received a six-month sentence for being an accessory to murder.

The Davis prosecution is in another league. The success of the case rests with

Jacobs's skill at unraveling the intricate and violent pattern of Davis's life.

While the defense will likely argue that Davis does not deserve a death sentence because he was too high on drugs to know what he was doing the night of the abduction, Jacobs will portray Davis as a calculating con who followed a familiar pattern of violence toward women. Davis has already confessed. He has led authorities to Polly's body. The physical evidence tied him to the crime. His history showed a pattern of cruelty. Now Jacobs must convince a jury that his theory about the Klaas crime is correct and the defense's argument for sympathy is off base.

"My theory is Davis was looking for an opportunity," Jacobs said. "He may have seen Polly get ice cream a few hours before the crime. In past crimes, Davis has said he had an urge to get a woman. He has made statements to psychologists about fantasizing about tying women up and sodomizing them."

"The satchel and the precut bindings Davis carried show a level of premeditation," Jacobs said.

"He has done all this before [in past crimes]," Jacobs said. "He is walking around with a bag with stuff in it. I call it his little assault kit."

Davis's past victims in Napa and Hayward

were also small women, Jacobs said. Both will be called as prosecution witnesses. Jacobs believes Davis chose Polly because she was dressed differently than Kate and Gillian and perhaps looked more mature in her halter top and short skirt.

"The other girls looked very young and they were dressed in baggy stuff," Jacobs said. "Polly looked older to him. He has referred to her as a broad [in the taped confession]. I think he blurred the line between teen and young woman."

Jacobs has consulted with FBI behavioral experts who can provide research that shows rapists often choose younger victims when they lose interest in older ones.

"The experts can say that suspects who have had a lack of success with older victims will go after younger and younger ones," Jacobs said. "Sometimes the interest can change from women to a younger victim. It is all part of their pathology."

If nothing else, Davis's criminal history shows his crimes became more violent as he aged.

Whether Davis had sex with Polly is unknown due to the decomposition of her body. Only Davis knows the truth and for now he denies the accusations. It is not likely Davis would admit such a claim since child molesters are the lowest form of life inside prison walls.

"Those who are convicted of child molestation or child killing are looked down upon by other inmates," Jacobs said. "Within his society a sex conviction on a child is the lowest blow of all. This is a blow to the macho idea these guys have about being able to get a woman on their own. He does not want to face that label."

But the sex accusation is crucial to Jacobs's theory of the case.

"I believe it is the motivation for the crime," Jacobs said. "Even if he thought he entered the house to steal, it seems every step he took disproves that and you are left with the theory he was going to do something bad to a female. He knew there were people in the home. He knew the place was occupied by young females. He walked in with a bag of bindings and he did not take anything for monetary gain. He took a child, we'd call her a girl, but in his mind he was taking a female and she appealed to his fantasies and desires."

Whether Davis actually consummated the sex act with his helpless victim can't be determined.

"I don't think he was able to have an orgasm [on Pythian Road]," Jacobs said. "I have been on the hill and it is extremely steep. He would have exerted himself getting up there [with her], so I doubt he was physically able to have sex with her."

Of course, the position of Polly's body and the fact her clothing was found untied and hitched up indicates something sexual could have occurred.

"I don't think he could have pulled her clothes to that position just by dragging her," Jacobs said.

To Jacobs, Davis is a life-long predator who tired of chasing older game, and like a wild animal, went after a tender child to satisfy an urge. The prosecutor must cover a great deal of rough ground before Davis is convicted.

"He [Davis] is the kind of guy who lives outside the normal conventions and rules of society," Jacobs said. "He is dangerous because he can disguise his true nature and lead people to believe he is a rational guy. A lot of people at the San Mateo half-way house thought he was a nice guy just down on his luck.

"He has a violent nature and a sex drive that has to be satisfied in these ways," Jacobs said. "Yet he is manipulative and can control his emotions and present himself as harmless. He has committed so many crimes of violence that he has exhausted his rights to remain in our society," Jacobs said. "He is happy in prison, so that is not a punishment. There is no reason for him to be around anymore."

Eleven

FOUR DAYS IN MAY

"The case leaves many of us with gnawing questions. Not everything has been answered."

Sonoma County Municipal Court Judge Robert P. Dale's courtroom was packed May 10, 1993 as Jacobs presented part of his case at the start of Davis's preliminary hearing. The hearing would serve as a mini-trial. The proceeding was less formal than a criminal trial and was held to show the court that investigators had enough evidence against Davis to warrant a full hearing before twelve jurors. The preliminary hearing gave prosecutors and defense attorneys a chance to view the evidence, to assess the witnesses and to check out the strength and weakness of a case.

Jacobs had hardly slept the night before. He knew Polly's friends Kate and Gillian would testify that day and he wasn't sure how the girls would handle the pressure of telling their terrible story in public with Davis staring at them as he sat a few paces away at the defense table. At least five sheriff's deputies stood about the room watching the audience. Dale didn't want any outbursts. The case would go by the book.

"It's important that the proceedings proceed in an orderly fashion," he said from the bench. "If there is any type of disturbance, they [deputies] are to deal with it immediately."

Members of Polly's family sat in the audience, most wore buttons bearing a picture of her smiling face. Davis wore a casual shirt and street clothes. You could not see his tattoos. Gone as well was his blue jailhouse jumpsuit and the chains dangerous inmates normally have latched to their feet and wrists. Davis's defense attorney, Barry Collins, had argued at an earlier hearing in March that the presence of jail garb and chains would have a prejudicial effect on Davis when seen by television viewers.

The court agreed and so when Davis walked into Dale's courtroom on May 10, he looked like any other member of the audience—just one more curious onlooker to the sad spectacle. But the relaxed attire was only fabric deep. The accused killer wore an electronic security device beneath his yellow dress shirt. One of the deputies in the courtroom watched Davis. If the inmate acted out, the deputy could deliver a powerful jolt with the touch of a button.

"It gives an electrical shock that can knock you right off your feet," Sonoma County Jail

Commander John Sully said, "We've tested it on our own staff and I can say it does what it's intended to do."

Davis wore the device around his waist. The electronic belt can deliver a 50,000-volt charge that sends shock waves through the back muscles and stops the wearer in his tracks. As it turned out, there was no need to use the device during the preliminary hearing. Everyone behaved quite well.

Eve Nichol was the first witness Jacobs called to the stand. She briefly outlined the events of that ill-fated night. She told Dale she was taking a bath when Kate arrived for Polly's slumber party.

"They were laughing and making girl-type noises," Nichol recalled of the girls' last night together.

She remembered being awakened by Kate after the suspect had stolen Polly and recalled the traumatized look on the young girl's face which prompted her to call 911. The young girls were next.

Dale barred the media from taking pictures of the witnesses. The *Santa Rosa Press Democrat* used a courtroom sketch artist to capture the setting. The dark-penciled artwork that appeared in the next day's newspaper looked antiquated in a world that had gotten used to live action via Court TV, and CNN's coverage of the Gulf War. Both young girls clutched stuffed animals as they took their turn on the witness stand. Each had to walk within a few feet of Davis before testifying. Oregon police sketch artist Jean Boylan, the woman who provided an extremely accurate wanted poster of the kidnap suspect after interviewing the twelve-year-olds, sat next to the girls through their testimony. Kate and Gillian were nervous but composed.

Gillian went first. She talked about the flannel nightgown she brought to the sleepover and about the white makeup the girls put on Polly's face. She remembered how Polly gasped when Davis walked into the bedroom and how the binding Davis used to tie the girls felt "soft and silky." She remembered how Polly cried and asked the stranger not to hurt her family. She told Dale the man who broke into the home that night did not scare her.

"I thought he didn't look mean or anything," she said. "It was like he had been outside peeling an apple with a knife. He didn't look mean or menacing."

Jacobs asked her to look around the courtroom and point out the suspect. She glanced toward Davis, who sat slouched in the chair with his head bent low.

"He's behind you to the left. He's wearing a light yellow shirt."

Collins did not question the girl.

Kate came next. She took the stand wearing a large lapel button with Polly's picture on it. She explained how the slumber party idea developed over lunch at the girls' junior high school. How she forgot about the party and went off to a soccer game, then begged her mother to take her to Polly's after Polly called to remind her about the fun event. She told Dale that she came dressed as a hippie but realized Polly and Gillian had beat her to the punch and had already dressed up as little animals. She remembered that Polly had complained that the kidnapper had tied her hands too tight and that the suspect had loosened the straps. She told the court the whole thing seemed like a joke that had gone a little too far.

"I don't know exactly what I thought," she said. "I didn't find it very funny, but at the same time I didn't think there was any real threat. I assumed it was a joke."

Jacobs asked her to point out the suspect. "I'm not positive, but I think he's sitting right there," she said, pointing to Davis.

Again, Collins let the girl leave without any cross examination.

Marc Klaas was the next witness sworn in. Before entering the courtroom, he told the *Press Democrat* that he had no desire to look at Davis. On the stand, Klaas glanced at the accused man as Klass told the court how he visited Polly every weekend. Klaas looked at Davis as he left the witness stand.

"It wasn't as bad as I thought it would be," he told the *Press Democrat*. "He made eye contact—more or less a blank stare. He can be a little intimidating. He's weird. He's just a punk."

Members of the Klaas family, including Joe Klaas, sat directly behind Davis during the hearing. One of Polly's aunts and Polly's grandmother cried while an FBI agent described the discovery of the girl's body. Evidence entered into the record on the first day of the preliminary hearing included a drawing of the knife authorities say Davis used to threaten the children. The actual weapon was never found. Authorities also presented the black sweatshirt found at Pythian Road, the strapping tape and condom found near Dana Jaffe's home, and a palm print found inside Polly's bedroom.

Petaluma Police Officer Larry Pelton took the stand in the afternoon of the first day. He told Dale how he processed evidence inside Klaas's Fourth Street home. He pointed out that pieces of a board game had been left scattered on Polly's bedroom floor and that the control cords on the girl's Nintendo game had been cut off.

FBI agent Anthony Maxwell came next. He had arrived at the Klaas home at about 5:30 A.M. the morning after the crime. Maxwell had been with the FBI for more than twelve years and specialized in collecting crime scene evidence. He explained how police tape had been set up outside the Klaas bungalow and how officers examined the home for fingerprints. They started in the rear of the home and moved up the back stairs and through the residence. Three dozen sets of prints were eventually found, Maxwell said.

The FBI used black and silver powder to raise and detect the prints. They also used a high-tech fluorescent red powder and an alternate light source to pick up prints that could not be seen with the naked eye. The light source puts out a high intensity beam that is emitted through a filter, which reflects images that can only be seen when investigators wear specialized glasses.

Maxwell said the investigative technique was similar to using a black light to illuminate invisible ink. The technique was used to locate a partial palm print matched to Davis that was found on the upper rail of Polly's bunk bed. Davis had apparently touched the bed with the ridge line of his palm, authorities believe. It was as if Davis had leaned against the railing. The partial palm print was the only one linked to Davis.

The FBI man shifted gears and told the court what he found at the Cloverdale site. He explained how the recovery team wore full-body white Tyvek environmental protection suits and masks as they wandered around the weed-covered berry patch. He said Polly's body was sandwiched between plywood and the berry bushes. The girl's skull and lower jaw had separated from the body and were found lying to the left of her remains. Her hair had separated from the skull and was found lying in the bushes.

FBI agent Charles Wilcox was there too. He explained how Polly's remains were placed in a body bag and taken to the coroner's office. He told Dale that Polly had been wearing a flannel nightgown over her blouse and short skirt. The nightgown had been pulled up above her waist and gathered under her armpits. The girl's underwear was torn and had decomposed. Wilcox could not say if the suspect had ripped the undergarments or if animals had eaten at them. He remembered that Polly's hands were folded over her body, right hand placed over the left.

Day one had been dramatic and graphic.

"I hate Richard Allen Davis," Marc Klaas told the *Los Angeles Times* after testifying. "But I don't put a lot of energy into thinking about him. He's a small man, a very, very small man."

The second day of testimony began with Polly's dentist, Robert Koenitzer, who had last seen the girl for a routine cleaning one month before the abduction.

Kate's mother came next. She recalled how

Polly called her home to persuade her into attending the slumber party. She said Polly sounded excited about the impending bash. She said she dropped her daughter off at about 8:00 P.M. and saw Polly and Gillian posing on the front steps of the Fourth Street house. She said a quick hello to Eve Nichol, then drove away. She told the court about seeing a man dressed in dark clothing walking around the neighborhood with a bag in his hand. She was unable to fully identify Davis as the man she saw that night.

"I'm not sure, it could be," McLean said.

Several neighbors took the stand May 11, and filled in details about the movements of the darkly dressed stranger they saw walking near Polly's home. Thomas George recalled eating hamburgers that night and seeing a suspect dressed in a long-sleeved shirt and boots passing Polly's house with a bag in his hand.

George, fourteen, identified Davis as the man he saw that night. Under cross examination from Collins, the youth admitted he picked a different person out of a line up in Ukiah after Davis's arrest. He said the suspect did not have a beard the night of the police lineup, which may have confused him.

Twelve-year-old Taleah Miller spoke about seeing a movie that night and returning to her home at 419 Fourth Street to find the darkly dressed figure walk by Polly's home. She remembered the man had a watch on his right hand and carried a bag in his left hand. She said the man's gray hair was not slicked down, but combed back.

"There are a lot of bums and stuff that walk down the street," she said. "I noticed him because he was just standing there and he wasn't doing anything."

Another FBI man, Chris Allen, a forensic lab specialist, explained how federal experts linked a fiber found in Polly's bedroom to the brown carpet inside Davis's Pinto hatchback. He also matched the edges of the silky cloth found at Polly's house to similar material found at Pythian Road and the Cloverdale site. Fibers lifted from the black sweatshirt found at Pythian Road matched the flannel nightgown that covered Polly's body.

The pieces of the puzzle were coming together. But the most dramatic moment of the second day of testimony came when Jaffe and her babysitter, Shannon Lynch, recounted their chilling encounter with Davis on Pythian Road. When asked if the frightening stranger she found stuck in the ditch was in the Dale's courtroom, Lynch choked up, but fixed her gaze at Davis.

"I see the person," she said. She glared at Davis as she left the stand, but he didn't look her way.

Dana Jaffe told her story as well. She told Dale how scared Lynch sounded on the phone when she called to warn her about the stranger found stuck on Pythian Road. She explained that two months· later, she found a pair of little girl's red tights, a man's sweatshirt, a condom, a book of matches, strips of packaging tape, a plastic six-pack holder and a piece of cloth on her land.

"Now Ms. Jaffe, I'd like you to look around the courtroom at this time," Jacobs began. "And I want to know if you see the person you encountered on the road that night, on the night of October 1, near the Pinto?"

"Yes sir, I do," she said.

"And could you describe what this person is wearing?" Jacobs asked.

"Yes, sir. He's wearing glasses and a yellow shirt, open at the collar."

"And he is seated at the table to my right?" Jacobs continued.

"Yes sir," she answered.

Sheriff's Deputy Mike Rankin, one of two Sonoma County officers who questioned Davis the night of the crime only to let him go because they were unaware of the kidnapping, told his side of the story. He explained how he was called to Pythian Road by Jaffe, who had found a trespasser on her land. How he questioned the man and put him through a sobriety check. How Davis tried to drink a beer in the deputies' presence.

"He opened it and I promptly told him he could not drink it in public," Rankin said.

He said Jaffe was given the option of making a citizen's arrest on Davis, but instead told the deputies to get the man off her land. He said Davis suggested the Sheriff's Department call a tow truck and pay for the tow. He also said the deputies could wait around while he called his brother-in-law in Ukiah who could drive down and help pull the car free.

"Eventually, I came up with a plan to get him out of the ditch," Rankin said.

Rankin recounted how he and fellow Deputy Thomas Michael Howard pulled the stuck Pinto from the ditch and sent Davis on his way. Rankin said he had to use his car's loudspeaker to order Davis to leave the area after his car was pulled free.

"He shrugged his shoulders and drove off down the road," Rankin told the court.

After two days of testimony it looked as if the prosecution had built a solid case of circumstantial evidence proving Davis had been in Polly's home the night she vanished. The physical evidence gathered at Pythian Road, from inside Davis's Pinto and at the Cloverdale site might be enough to bring a conviction. Now it was Petaluma Police Sgt. Mike Meese's turn to put the icing on the cake.

On the third day of testimony, Meese gave a narrative account of Davis's lengthy taped confession, which proved Davis committed the crime, but left many doubts as to when Polly actually died, or why Davis took her in the first place. The May 13, 1993 testimony marked the first public airing of Davis's account. A hushed courtroom listened to Meese as he summarized in an hour, his long interview with Davis, who sat rigidly at the defense table while Meese spoke.

Davis had "no idea" why he picked Polly's house and didn't know why he took Polly away, according to Meese's testimony. When Meese questioned Davis about trying to have sex with the girl, the suspect quickly denied the allegation.

"As much as I remember I didn't try to have sex with her," Davis told Meese. "On my skin, I didn't do nothing to her."

Davis then told Meese, "You guys [will] soon find that out."

Different people have interpreted Davis's statement in various ways. The prosecution contends the statement shows Davis knew an autopsy would reveal he had tried to sexually assault the girl. The defense believes otherwise. The point is significant since the

charge of attempted sexual assault is one of
the special allegations needed to sway a jury
toward the death penalty.

At trial, the prosecution is expected to
build a case of attempted sexual assault
around the condom found at Pythian Road
and the fact that Polly's clothing had been
pushed up in a manner consistent with a
rape. Jacobs had said Davis covered Polly in
the flannel nightgown because the garment
fit in with some sort of sexual fantasy he
had developed. Collins will likely argue that
there is no evidence linking Davis to the
Rough Rider condom found on Jaffe's property.

"The mere presence of an item which can
be used for sexual contact does not mean
that a sexual crime occurred," defense attorney Collins stated in court documents.

Collins has also taken issue with the notion
Davis had fantasies about the attack.

"The prosecution has said the nightgown
was part of a fantasy designed for maximum
sexual gratification," Collins stated in court
papers. "The fantasy which is alleged exists
not in the evidence, but in the fantasies of
the People and their illusions of this case."

Whether Davis tried to rape the girl may
never be known. When Polly died may also
remain a mystery.

Davis told Meese he untied the girl after
getting stuck on Pythian Road.

"I put her on the hill and told her to be quiet because my car was stuck," Davis said, according to Meese's testimony.

Investigators say it is more likely Polly remained bound, hooded and gagged during the entire encounter on Pythian Road. Meese recounted how Davis retrieved Polly from the hillside.

"She was asleep," he told Meese. "She was laying there all curled up."

Meese told how Polly reportedly expressed worry that he "had left her," and how they traveled off together toward Cloverdale. As they drove north along Highway 101 Polly kept asking to go home. Davis kept saying he'd take her there soon, according to Meese. Davis claimed he waited by the Cloverdale site for almost an hour thinking over his options. He said Polly needed to use the restroom, and they walked away from the Pinto together.

He strangled her with a piece of cloth that was found on her body. It was still tied in a knot when investigators discovered it. He even made a hand gesture to show how he committed the act by looping his fists over an imaginary victim and pulling the rope tight, according to court documents. Davis told Meese that he didn't know how long it [death] would take, so he picked up a piece of white cloth he found on the ground and tied it tightly around her.

"I tied it around her neck, cinched up the neck, tightened it up just to make sure," Davis said. "She didn't know what hit her."

Outside Dale's courtroom, Polly's family gathered to talk about the rough testimony. They gave little credence to Davis's story about Polly patiently waiting for him to return to Pythian Road.

"I don't believe for a second my granddaughter was waiting for the law [deputies] to go away so she could be picked up by that monster," Joe Klaas said. "She wouldn't take any baloney."

Judge Dale felt the same way and told Davis so when court resumed May 13. After listening to twenty-four witnesses over the past three days of testimony, Dale was convinced there was ample evidence to hold Davis for trial on charges ranging from murder, kidnapping, false imprisonment, and assault with intent to commit a lewd act on a child. He delivered a harsh five-minute speech while Davis stood motionless.

Dale had his own theory about the crime. He concluded that Davis— having seen Kate's mother leave Polly's house by car— suspected no adults were in the residence. He didn't believe Davis chose the bungalow at random, or that Davis was too drunk on beer or high on PCP-laced marijuana to know what he was doing.

"This is not a person who is intoxicated

or confused," Dale said from the bench. "This is a person who has a plan, who has a design. This is a person who continued to carry it out."

Had Davis been high on drugs, investigators say the Sonoma County deputies would have detected signs of intoxication when they examined Davis on Pythian Road. Dale agreed.

"His statements that he did not remember [taking Polly] borders on the absurd," Dale said. "And the court gives no credence to it whatsoever."

Dale also agreed with the prosecution that there was evidence Davis tried to rape his young victim.

"The body was partially unclothed, her clothing was pushed up above her waist, her blouse was untied and white skirt was inside out," Dale lectured. "The court can't believe that all, I repeat, that all of that clothing came to be in that position because of her simply being dragged into the bush. It simply doesn't make sense."

But some key questions remained unanswered.

"The case leaves many of us with gnawing questions," Dale said. "Not everything has been answered. Was Polly Klaas alive at Pythian Road? When did she die? How did she die? I don't know. I don't think any of us knows, except for one person, Polly Klaas. [And she] can't tell us."

As for Davis's statements that he let the girl rest on a hillside on Pythian Road, Dale had this to say:

"I can't believe the rest of it," the judge began. "It borders on the absurd, and it appears to me to be insane, inconsequential, inconsistent, incongruous; just makes no sense whatsoever. It does not make sense that after half an hour she would still be there. It doesn't make sense. I do not believe that whatever her condition, that Polly Klaas was able, [to be] sleeping on a hill, [or] was conscious at all."

Davis stood at attention as Dale ordered him to stand trial. Marc Klaas sat with his head bowed during the thirty-minute hearing. As Dale reached his opinion, Marc clutched hands with Meese. Outside the court, defense attorney Collins said he would consider a plea bargain if the district attorney agreed not to seek a death penalty.

"We might be able to work something out," he told the *Press Democrat*.

That wasn't going to happen.

"If there ever is a case that deserves the death penalty, it's the Davis case," Jacobs told the Santa Rosa paper.

Twelve

PETALUMA 1994

"I should not be standing here. This little girl did not have to die."

On the outside, Petaluma looked the same in October 1994 as it had one year before. Locals said hello to tourists who window-shopped outside the town's many antique stores. A local bakery had onion bread on sale. A banner stretched across the main drag reminding locals about the upcoming Wristwrestling Championship that was only a week away on October 8.

Richard Lieb was once again standing outside the main post office raising money for blind kids.

The downtown streets were busy on October 1, 1994 as a children's day festival was in full swing. Kids roamed all over the place, gleefully grabbing balloons from men dressed to look like Power Rangers.

Walnut Park was a place of joy. Toddlers scrambled across the grass while mothers watched and gossiped. Young kids pushed themselves skyward on swing sets. Fall was upon Sonoma County. The air was crisp, the trees were changing color.

Like the foliage, Petaluma was adjusting, carrying on and trying to forget the tragedy that occurred only one year before. But the media had come to town once more to update the world about the Petaluma miracle and Polly power and all the rest.

Dallas will always be stained by the events of November 22, 1963. Memphis will never escape the bullet fired by James Earl Ray, and Petaluma, despite its small-town atmosphere and pleasant history, will always carry a purple scar.

Richard Allen Davis remained inside the Sonoma County Jail in Santa Rosa a year after the crime, while his defense attorney argued for a change of venue. The *Santa Rosa Press Democrat* marked the Polly Klaas anniversary with a page-one story detailing attorney Barry Collins's plans. Collins had commissioned a phone interview of prospective jurors and concluded there was no chance his client could get a fair trial in Sonoma County.

"Everyone knows virtually everything that's been reported about the case thus far, including his [Davis's] confession and his prior criminal record," Collins told the press. "The overwhelming majority think he's guilty."

Collins said he conducted a similar phone survey in two Bay Area counties and one in Southern California and found better results. Jacobs conducted a survey of his own that showed Davis could get a fair hearing in the community where the crime took place.

Davis fueled the media machine in August 1994 when he filed a claim against the Sonoma County Jail for confiscating $1.45 in stamps from his cell.

"We are looking into the matter," said Sonoma County Sheriff Mark Ihde. "It's going to cost a whole lot more in paperwork than the stamps are worth."

The dispute died four days later when an anonymous donor gave the accused killer five postage stamps. Davis drew attention again in September 1994 when he called *Santa Rosa Press Democrat* reporter James W. Sweeney to complain about jail conditions. True to his habit of admitting guilt when questioned, Davis told Sweeney he had killed Polly Klaas, but denied molesting the twelve-year-old.

"I was messed up," Davis told the paper. "They [prosecutors] don't want to believe that. I bought a joint off a dude and got more than I bargained for. There was no premeditation [to the crime], no intent."

Davis said the whole thing would never have happened had he been able to find his mother that fated night.

"I made a mistake of buying a quart of beer," he told Sweeney. "As I was walking back to the 7-Eleven I met the homeless dudes. I bought the weed. It's just all this other stuff they're trying to stick me with. Like one guy said to me, it's like cooking spaghetti. You throw it at the wall and see what sticks."

Davis, who spends all but one hour a day inside a cell equipped with a toilet, bunk, sink and writing desk, said the political fall-out from the crime shocked him.

"All this hoopla," he told the newspaper. "Even the president. Everybody jumped on this. It helps them out. I was very surprised, but, hey, politicians are politicians."

Davis spoke with Sweeney for fifteen minutes, but refused to answer key questions dealing with when Polly was killed. He had called the press to complain about being housed in an area reserved for mentally ill inmates. The place was too loud, he told the paper.

"There's no point having someone else's mental instability inflicted onto mine," he told Sweeney. "I don't have any to begin with."

A year after Polly's murder, Eve Nichol kept her mental composure through meditation.

She moved away from the town long ago. She had gone into seclusion, avoided press interviews and sought spiritual guidance through reading and friends. She now lived in Napa County with Annie and her husband Allan.

"My life this past year has been a quiet and contemplative one," Nichol wrote in the *Marin Independent*. "I've spent a great deal of time with my children and family. I've reconnected with old friends and have been blessed with new friends who have deeply enriched my life."

She got involved with a Petaluma Theater group called The Rising Star Playhouse, and helped the membership restore a vintage church which was renamed the Polly Hannah Klaas Arts Center.

"I've done a great deal of reading, writing and meditation, which help to quiet my mind and hopefully see my way more clearly," she wrote in the *Independent*. "There are so many ways of reaching out, of giving something back in return for this life. If everyone would just do something to leave this place a little better than we found it. Maybe we can't do great things, but we can strive to do small things with great love."

Eve was trying to move on.

So were the occupants of the home Polly once played in on Fourth Street. A new family had arrived about six months after the crime. The neighbors were glad someone brought the place back to life. By October 1994, the new tenants had grown tired of the gawkers who occasionally stop by to look at the spot where a notorious crime took place. A young man who now lives in the bungalow did not want to talk about the year-old story. He didn't give his name to reporters, but said people still send flowers to the house.

"I can't accept them," the new tenant, a Fairfax native, told the *Marin Independent*. "It's not fair to the neighbors to be constantly reminded of it. They've been through enough."

Of course, so had Marc Klaas.

"Marc is totally different," his father Joe Klaas said. "Before he was happy go lucky, fun loving. He was a humorous fellow."

Marc married his longtime girlfriend, Violet Cheer in June 1994. At the wedding the couple wore buttons bearing Polly's name. He gave up his Hertz rental business in San Francisco long ago.

"I can't see myself telling people how to get to the 17 Mile Drive anymore," Klaas said, referring to a popular scenic route for tourists. "I've got to help kids."

Marc started his own foundation. He had become frustrated by the restrictions of the Polly Klaas Foundation, which focused on helping to find missing children and could not undertake lobbying efforts. As a non-profit organization, the Polly Klaas Foundation could only devote 25 percent of its money toward lobbying. Marc wanted to go after the politicians on his own. He started the Marc Klaas Foundation for Children in late September 1994 to focus on stopping habitual violent offenders—through legislation and education.

"I have a personal agenda," he told the media. "This is for myself and the memory of my daughter."

He reported on the Susan Smith murder case for the television show "American Journal" after the Union County South Carolina woman admitted drowning her two young sons. In August, Marc's brother Jonathan died of complications from AIDS. Before he died, the 35-year-old man told his parents about Polly, according to a report in *People* magazine. The dying man told his father, Joe Klaas, "Dad, Polly came to me. I swear to God," the magazine reported. "I said, 'Polly, why do you have such tiny wings?' And she said, 'Because I wasn't ready to go yet. But Johnny, you're ready, and you're going to have great big wings.' "

In the dream, Polly told her uncle that she hasn't seen heaven yet, but that she'll get there, riding with him. Jonathan Klaas died three days after reporting the dream to his family.

1993-94 had been the worst of times for the family Klaas.

But the Polly Klaas Foundation's future looked bright. Volunteers greeted the anni-

versary of Polly's abduction with the hopes
of creating an endowment fund that would
keep it active for years to come. The foundation received $550,000 in donations follow-
ing Polly's abduction. The endowment would
serve as a savings account, preserving future
donations and hopefully keep volunteers
busy helping other lost kids well into the
next century. Since Polly's death, the foundation had become a model for other communities to follow.

National publicity from the case led fifteen
states to adopt sex-offender registries to help
law enforcement and community members
know where paroled sex criminals were living.

As the anniversary of his daughter's murder approached, Marc urged friends and
families to spend the day with their own children. That, he said would be a fitting tribute
to Polly. Many took his advice, but others,
especially those who had followed the case
closely, had worked in the Polly Klaas Center, or had helped search for the missing
child, grieved in the open. Some went to
Petaluma Junior High School and gazed
upon the children's mural dedicated to Polly.
Others drove north to Cloverdale and walked
amid the newly planted flowers. They
planted violets, said prayers, lit candles and
left messages in a guest registration book
that hung from a pole shoved into the

ground steps away from where the girl's body was found one year before.

A plastic bag covered the book to protect it from the weather. A pen on a chain hung nearby. Dozens of people stopped by the shrine to honor a girl many had never seen. They drove slowly toward the Cloverdale garden, parked their cars and gently walked upon the now sacred ground. Their steps were soft and quiet. Most did not speak as they paced amid the wildflowers and candles before the shrine. Other folks drove past the Cloverdale site on Highway 101 and honked their horns to show they cared.

Eight of Polly's friends spent hours walking about the abandoned lumber mill. They lit candles and incense. They signed the registration book and walked about the site with their arms slung over one another's shoulders. The mood was somber. None wanted to talk. Each asked a photographer from the *San Francisco Examiner* to give them space and peace. The photographer relented even though the girls made a strong visual image as they knelt before a purple cross bearing Polly's picture.

Steve Connolly, the retired Cloverdale band teacher, showed up as usual. He carried a plastic water jug and gave the newly planted flowers a drink, lit his pipe and pondered the tragic story.

The mourners kept coming as the afternoon drifted toward dusk. Many wore purple ribbons pinned to their lapels, others had buttons with Polly's beaming face stuck to their jackets and shirts.

The Petaluma Junior High School girls wore Polly Klaas T-shirts, as if they were members of an exclusive team. The shirts had a blooming rose on the front. The words, "We love you Polly" rested beneath the vivid flower. Everyone hugged, and cried.

Adults sat on wooden park benches and stared at the crosses, the flowers, the burning candles and wept.

Polly Klaas Center volunteer Lee Praught spent two hours at the site. She dabbed at eyes welled up with tears even as she planted a tree and an African violet to honor the dead girl. The tree had been left at the Polly Klaas Center months before and had taken a turn for the worse. Praught had kept the tree in her yard where it grew strong. Today she decided it belonged closer to Polly. Praught, a mother of three, had joined the Polly Klaas movement early on during the search days and stayed to the terrible end. She first came to the Cloverdale site in the spring of 1993 to plant wildflowers and bulbs. This was her first trip back since that spring day.

"It is a place to come and reflect," she said. "It was once ugly, it's not ugly anymore.

Polly symbolized the little girl in me. We tried hard to find her and bring her home safe. It is sad we did not do her any good, but through her death good is being done for other children."

Like thousands of other Petaluma volunteers, Praught held out hope that Polly Klaas would make it out alive, that somehow the plucky little girl could beat the odds and come back.

"It [the search] became an all-consuming thing," Praught said. "You did not think a negative thought. We were not going to let that happen."

Praught's husband Don Harvey, another center volunteer had mixed feelings about the Cloverdale site.

"It is a place where a little girl was dumped," he said, while his wife went off to plant her offerings. "But when you look at what the people of Cloverdale have done here, it shows they really care. It is their personal memorial."

Lynn Mills, another center volunteer, said many people joined the search effort after seeing video tapes of Polly on television.

"That brought Polly to life," she said. "This is what made Polly alive in most people's eyes. For me, right up until the point where they dragged her away from here [Cloverdale] you could not convince me that she was gone. I put my heart and soul in this. There is something wrong with the world."

Mills comes to the shrine once or twice a month, when her emotions are strong enough to stand the site's power. On the anniversary date, she is wavering on the edge of tears.

"I should not be here standing here," she says. "This little girl did not have to die. This guy was a kidnapper and rapist, everyone knew. He should not have been let loose."

At sunset, the *Examiner* photographer packed up his gear and headed south toward the Bay. He had gotten some good shots, but not the ones he had hoped for. Moments later, Marc Klaas, his sister Maureen, and Polly's grandparents Joe and B.J. pulled to a stop.

"Don't ask them any questions, please," Praught said. "They are family."

Marc carried a bouquet of red roses in his arms. He wore a purple warm-up jacket that bore Polly's name. With Violet Cheer at his side, he approached the candles and the crosses, which mark the spot where investigators uncovered her remains.

The couple lit lavender candles and placed them beneath a sign that hung over the shrine. It reads: "For a brief time an angel rested here." Joe Klaas put a hand on his son's shoulder, B.J. held his hand. Moments later, Marc and Violet sat before the burning candles and pressed their heads together in meditation.

He later walked around the garden, looking at the registration book, reading the thoughts other mourners had left behind. He knelt before a red, heart-shaped sign that also decorates the shrine and put his hands on his head. Next he moved to the cross that carries a picture of his smiling child in her dotted sweater. He stared at it in silence.

Joe Klaas, meanwhile, worked the small crowd of friends and volunteers who had been at the shrine for hours. He greeted them all, shook their hands and made small talk. Occasionally one could hear his deep laugh. He was cordial to all and took time to chat with two French journalists in town to film a documentary about violence in America. The pair had tried to interview Davis and his attorney Barry Collins, but the defense lawyer declined the offer.

Joe Klaas, always a friend to the media, always ready to share a story, motioned the cameraman close as he knelt in the dirt that marked the spot where his granddaughter once lay. He asked several of those gathered to move their cars and turn on their headlights so the cameraman could shoot the scene as daylight gave way to night. As the car lights sent beams toward the shrine, Joe Klaas told the sad story of a twelve-year-old-girl, who played the clarinet and did a mean impersonation of Elvis.

Marc Klaas grew weary of the scene. He left behind a note.

"Thank you for being the community that went beyond and did everything possible to help find Polly," he wrote, "I'll always cherish your letters, poems, songs and artwork and kind words and positive thoughts. You are the heroes the world is looking for."

He and Violet embraced and walked away from the candles they had lit and the flowers they had left. They got into their car and drove home. As the tragic figures moved amid the flickering candlelight, Don Harvey glanced westward and smiled. The sun had already set and the sky had turned a gentle shade of purple.

Thirteen

END GAME

"I fully expect to be standing in San Quentin with Marc when Davis finally meets his end."

Richard Allen Davis has spent more than a year inside the Sonoma County Jail. The surroundings are nothing new for him. He gets mail and on occasion answers letters. He watches television and talks to his sister's attorney, Erik R. Petersen, who says Davis is quite calm about his upcoming trial. After all, the criminal justice system has been Davis's foster parent for most of his life.

"He knows the system," Petersen said. "He knows it is out of his hands. He knows it may be years and years before he may face execution and he may have information to dump at trial. My gut feeling tells me there is something more to this case than meets the eye."

Petersen said Davis even has female admirers who write him. Davis even finds some humor in that.

"He jokes about having women write him letters from across America wanting to marry him," Petersen said. "He laughs about it. To him it is amusing and funny. When it comes right down to it, I don't know if he is crazy. My gut says that you can't do what he is alleged to have done and not be crazy, but he still views other people as crazy."

Davis is expected to face trial for the murder of Polly Klaas in June 1995. The trial may last six months. More than 200 witnesses may be called to testify. It will be a legendary spectacle, but it will not have a tabloid taint. But there will be no media circus, or post-trial commentary by media personalities. The hunt for Polly may have captured the nation's heart, but most people will not have the stomach for nightly reviews of the facts surrounding her death.

Backed with Davis's reported confession, FBI evidence, the palm print and eye witnesses' accounts, the main issue at trial will not be who killed Polly Klaas, but how Davis will be punished. Sonoma County tends to be a bit more liberal than other parts of California. It is hard to say how the jury will swing. The panel may take pity on Davis and reason society is better off having him jailed for life, rather than having him placed on a slow-track trip to the gas chamber. Defense attorney Barry Collins will certainly do his best to fight for his client's life by raising as many mitigating facts about the accused child killer as he can. Prosecutor Greg Jacobs will paint Davis as a wolf in human clothing, who has preyed on the helpless all his life. No one will emerge from the battle feeling good. Death penalty cases take their toll on all who enter the judicial arena.

Jacobs, though somewhat liberal on many issues, comes down in favor of executions. Putting killers in the death seat does not bother him. He does, however, have trouble with the fact that it takes thirteen to fifteen years to carry the death sentences out.

"The only problem I have with the system is that there is such a delay before there is an execution," Jacobs said. "I wonder if that is appropriate. It loses its value when you drag it out like that. It is said that the death penalty is a way for orderly people to deal with revenge. It permits the system of justice to substitute for the ancient technique of eye for eye and tooth for tooth. We say that it is our way of dealing with feeling of revenge for the victims, but we delay the penalty for 13 years. In that amount of time the person convicted may have changed a lot and have change their personality, so you are not executing the same person in a sense. That might be a strong argument for cruel and unusual punishment."

Jacobs favors swift justice.

"There is place for it," he said. "After having seen how much human suffering can be caused by people. And there are people who do crimes then adjust well to prison. So in that sense there is no real punishment for them for doing something terrible. There has to be this ultimate penalty."

The murder trial was supposed to start in March 1995, but Collins sought a delay to undergo serious dental work.

Collins can't go to trial with loose dentures, Jacobs said, so the delay has been granted. Jacobs expects to spend the summer picking a jury to hear the case. The matter will go before Superior Court Judge Lawrence "Gary" Antolini, who once served as Jacob's superior in the District Attorney's Office.

The national media will likely not swarm the courtroom and provide nightly updates. Antolini has been lukewarm to allowing cameras inside the courtroom. Jacobs expects little sensation. He points out that the case is not a "who done it."

"The publicity has sort of died off," Jacobs said. "I don't see a lot of media interest. I would be surprised if people are lined up to get in to see the trial."

Davis's pattern of violence will be highlighted during the trial. Jacobs plans to call old girlfriends and past crime victims to court to trace the accused killer's bloody trail from La Honda to Petaluma.

"Davis has not been out in the [real] world since he was twenty," Jacobs said. "He may not know how to relate to women. To him a thirteen-year-old may be the same as a twenty-five-year-old, as long as she is attractive."

Jacobs will tell the jury that primal urges drove Davis to murder. That urge coupled with Davis's inability to cope with life outside of a jail cell proved a potent mix that ended in Polly's death, he believes.

"He is a predator who lives on the edge, like a wolf that picks victims out of a herd," Jacobs said. "He is someone who has gotten to the point where he has a need or urge to pick off a woman, girl, who fits his image and satisfies his desires."

Joe Klaas, and other members of Polly's family will be in the courtroom when they bring Davis to justice.

"Davis is an anti-social psychopath who is legally sane," Joe Klaas said. "He is a loner. He goes around and waits to hurt people. When you have a child kidnapped, you hope someone is taking care of the child. But these types of stalkers are only interested in sex. They steal the child to murder the child. It is the killing that gets them off."

Joe Klaas now lectures around the state spreading the word about his granddaughter. He hopes new laws can be passed to protect other children from similar fates. Somehow he has kept faith in a higher order.

"I don't believe God is responsible for people who don't put themselves in the care of

God, and very few people do," Joe Klaas said. "Really good people get hurt. I don't blame God for what happens on this planet. The planet is run by human beings. The trouble with the world at large may be that we, not God, took charge."

Many tied to the investigation and the crime turn spiritual when asked to ponder the meaning of what could be learned from so senseless a crime.

Mike Meese, the veteran Petaluma Police detective whose cool head and respectful treatment of Davis helped secure a confession, put it this way:

"I am a firm believer in God and God does not give us anymore than we can handle. These things are given to learn and grow from. I could be a blubbering idiot in the corner thinking about the tragedy," he said. "We learn that this is the first time there was a unified effort between FBI and police department and the community joined in. And look, we solved it. They have not solved any of the other child abduction cases."

Mainly, Meese said, society must protect its children. Marc Klaas has the same view. He has become a familiar face in the media and has become nearly obsessed with the need to avenge his daughter's murder by protecting other children.

"My advice to parents is to raise your children as if there is a registered sex offender living in your neighborhood," he told the *Los Angeles Times*.

He hopes to build the Marc Klaas Foundation for Children into a long-lasting effort, with crime prevention videos and a nationwide newsletter. For now, the organization struggles to stay afloat. A crime summit he once planned never took place. Yet, his daughter's memory is everywhere. He wears buttons that carry her picture wherever he travels. The *Los Angeles Times* reported that he celebrated her birthday by dining on her favorite meal, teriyaki chicken.

"Everything I see reminds me of my daughter," he told the *Times*. "Every time I turn around I see her. I have sadness followed by profound anger that chases me through my days."

The anger will stay with Klaas for years to come, especially if Davis is convicted and receives a death sentence. Should that day come, Klaas will likely face Davis once again. He won't be alone.

"I fully expect to be standing in San Quentin with Marc when Davis finally meets his end," Meese said. "I expect to be there. I would not go for my own personal satisfaction, that is not something I would want to go to my maker with on my conscience, but I think I will probably go for Marc."

Though Marc Klaas and the Polly Klaas

Foundation parted ways, the organization that sprouted in the wake of the tragedy continues its journey. The foundation has assisted in searches for more than 130 missing and abducted children and has lobbied for the passage of laws to strengthen sentencing requirements for serious and violent felons.

Not only has the Polly Klaas Foundation become a watchdog agency for missing children, but the Justice Department has since developed a manual to guide police agencies how to deal with similar crimes. The guidelines recommend law enforcement agencies broadcast new reports of missing children over all police frequencies and that they file missing children reports with the FBI's National Crime Information Center.

Petaluma Police Captain Pat Parks has taken the lessons learned in the case and lectured to dozens of other police organizations around the state. FBI agent Mark Mershon said the investigation fueled his agency as well, and led to the creation of a crimes against children task force. The techniques learned and perfected by FBI agents during the murder investigation are being applied to unsolved child abduction cases and may, Mershon said, lead to new arrests.

"There is a lot of good and evil in the world and there is always a balance," Parks said. "God puts us on the planet and we make choices, some make good ones, others bad ones. God has a way of taking the bad choices people make and showing us the benefit of the good. He showed us a piece of evil and what evil can do. He points the meaning and value of those choices. God takes those situations and makes something special. God takes, there is sacrifice. So here is this little innocent girl and God allowed that to happen and I don't know why. But I know we can make something good come from it. Marc Klaas was hawking cars out of a motel and was a nobody. Now he has turned into a crusader for some good things. Look at all the lives Polly touched. Their kids became more special to them and we are focused on the evil that is out there. Love was present every step of the way. The love of Marc for his daughter, the love they had for their family. If you look past the bad there was so much good. Polly died for the next little girl and the next one. Hopefully we can prevent others and that will give her life meaning."

Fourteen

GRANDPA JOE

"You put the politicians on one side of the room and the reporters on the other and ask yourself, which side are the crooks on?"

Joe Klaas was never one to shy away from a fight. He battled Pete Wilson and Dan Lungren when he thought they used his granddaughter's death for political gain. He challenged the Petaluma cops and hired private investigators because he thought the police were slack. At seventy-four years of age, Joe Klaas is as feisty as they come.

Today, Joe Klaas does not look much like the steely nerved fighter pilot who shot down two enemy planes in World War II before landing in a POW camp and helping plan an escape. Nowadays, he resembles Las Vegas comedian Foster Brooks, with his wavy gray hair, slight paunch and aristocratic white beard. And like the comic who built a career spoofing a drunkard, Polly's grandfather uses jokes and a deep laugh to break tension or enhance the telling of a tale.

He jokes with everyone and behaves like a joyous host whether he greets reporters at Polly's shrine, or inside his small Carmel office decorated with packed bookshelves and pictures of the planes he flew during the war. He smiles a lot for a man who has seen so bright a family star snuffed out so early in life. But Klaas has seen lots of rough times in his life.

Klaas saw Central Europe from behind the barbed-wire fence of prisoner-of-war camp Luft Stalag Three, and an adventure that became known as "The Great Escape." Every American boy who ever held a GI Joe action figure knows the story by heart thanks to the 1963 blockbuster film starring Steve McQueen and James Garner. The movie, based on the book by Klaas's POW mate, Roger Bickle, told the story of brave Allied prisoners carving secret tunnels in the frozen Polish soil, then making a break for freedom. Six hundred were supposed to get out. Only seventy-six made it through before the tunnel was discovered. Fifty of the escapees were caught, lined up, shot and cremated by the Germans. Most of the others were caught and returned. A handful escaped to neutral countries.

Klaas saw it all. He served on the camp's escape committee. But he never reached the tunnel itself. After camp guards found one of the escape tunnels, all the imprisoned American troops were moved to a different compound.

Klaas went into the media after the war,

did a radio show with his wife B.J. in Anchorage, worked as an account executive for a San Francisco radio station, wrote nine books and raised six kids. Two of his books, novels about World War II, have been printed in Dutch and proved popular in Holland.

"I've been a reporter, and an author, so I am not afraid of the media," Klaas said. "You put the politicians on one side of the room and the reporters on the other and ask yourself which side are the crooks on?"

After Polly was taken, Klaas opened himself up to the media and said reporters kept the story alive. He had less faith in those who tried to find the missing girl. At first, he saw a massive conspiracy behind the kidnapping. He speculated in public that Davis had acted on behalf of others. Eventually, he realized the cops were right, at least about Davis.

"My theories are not worth much," Klaas said as he sat back and laughed. "I did more god-damned investigating than anyone else. I had 200 cops from New York and 50 private eyes. I investigated the satanic cults and the child auctions, everything you could imagine. I didn't find a damn thing."

Klaas lives in a two-bedroom Carmel home with B.J. Polly used to visit them often. When Klaas talked about selling the place, she'd always shoot the idea down.

"You can't sell this place, all my memories are here," the little girl would say.

Now those memories haunt the cottage's occupants.

"It's kind of sad living here," Klaas said. "Last spring my dog Pucci died. He was the same age as Polly. I went on the back porch one day and found Pucci lying on the porch. He was cold. I like to say that Polly called him."

A POEM
BY
JOE KLAAS

My Polly's face smiles out at me
from every window that I see

The dimpled grace of the sweet face
still follows me from place to place

The wonder of her missing smile
is that it lasts mile after mile

She isn't lost without a trace
as long as I see Polly's face.

Afterword

THE POLITICS OF POLLY

"The only thing we can do as a memorial for Polly Klaas is to see she is the last child to suffer."

Those unfamiliar with the mechanics of American justice might not understand how a man like Davis could get out of prison time and time again despite his long record. It wasn't by smart lawyering, since Davis was his own worst enemy in many cases. He almost always confessed to his deeds and took his punishment without much complaint. He fooled no one and even told a judge he did bad things because he felt like it.

It wasn't because of sympathy. Every judge he came up against gave him the maximum sentence. Every police officer or sheriff's deputy he crossed knew Davis was a bad seed. Every psychiatrist who looked into Davis's black eyes saw the evil that swirled behind his calm face and thought he belonged away from society. And still he walked free from extensive prison sentences and managed to commit new crimes, each more foul than the last.

How could it be?

The answer lay in the way California lawmakers grew wary of judges and the citizens
who sat upon parole boards. To understand
the tragedy, one must travel back in time to
the mid-1970s. In those days judges had
more authority and were allowed to analyze
the defendants that came before the bench.
They would hear the accused tell a tale, review the suspect's good and bad qualities,
examine the circumstances of the crime in
question and hand down a sentence.

If a suspect received a life term, as Davis
did for his crime spree in Napa, the inmate
would sit in prison for years with his only
hope for salvation coming from the arbitrary
pleasure of the parole board. Davis had been
before several parole hearings and had always been turned down. Had the law not
changed, Davis might have remained in
prison, starting as far back as 1977.

But a change came in the mid-1970s, when
California did away with the existing system
and set up a new sentencing method that
limited the power of judges and parole
boards. Now all crimes would be calibrated
along a running scale that set a specific
length of sentence for each offense. The
scale included a high, middle and low range
that took into account some for the facts of
each case. An inmate could get a slightly
longer sentence if the crime was aggravated,
or a few less years if there were extenuating

circumstances behind the deed. If the case was typical, the judge chose the middle term and that was that. Though the sentences might have sounded impressive when announced in court, they were much softer in practice since the new method allowed prisoners to earn good-time credits. In most cases, inmates cut their sentences in half by behaving behind bars.

The retooling was a blessing for Davis, who saw his life term reduced before he walked free in 1982. The same system ushered him to the exit door once more in 1993.

But in 1994 the winds of change—kicked up by election year politics—were swirling. Davis and Polly Klaas were at the center of the storm that gave rise to crime reform. California state was embarking on a crueler and less gentle path toward criminals. And before it ended, hundreds of low-level street toughs would awaken to a new order. The days of reform and coddling were over for those who could not get prison out of their blood.

Polly Klaas and Kimber Reynolds, served as poster children to the cause. Both died violently at the hands of brutal men. Taken together their stories were more than the state could stomach. Crime, especially violent crime, had become one of the top issues in the state. With newspapers and television news shows filling their pages and screens with crime stories, the state had become obsessed with crime in the 1990s. The video-taped beating of Rodney King was hard enough to look at, but the riots that followed in 1992 set the state on edge. Little did it matter that drive-by shootings seemed largely confined to metropolitan areas, crime became a worry for people from Encinitas, in San Diego County, to towns like Eureka near the border with Oregon.

Californians had spent months reading about young Polly. In the months that followed her death, they heard just as much about Davis and other career criminals who used the lax prison system to escape true justice. Everyone's blood was up and the state wanted answers. By the time the Klaas family scattered Polly's ashes in the Pacific, the state had a new rallying cry. Soon many of the same people who had devoted their lives to finding the missing Klaas girl had a new cause as they chanted their new mantra: "Three Strikes and You're Out."

The tough anti-crime idea did not rise from Polly's grave. A year before Polly's abduction, the plan had been brought before the state Legislature by another father who lost his daughter in an equally senseless crime. Few people noticed its significance until Davis struck. But Mike Reynolds noticed a need for judicial reform, even if no one else did.

Unlike the scene at Polly Klaas's memorial,

there were no pop artists singing for Mike and Sharon Reynolds in the summer of 1992 after an armed man grabbed their daughter Kimber's purse then put a bullet in her brain. Kimber Reynolds was an 18-year-old student at the Fashion Institute of Design and Marketing in Los Angeles. She had come home to Fresno in June 1992 for a high school friend's wedding. While on her way for dessert at the Daily Planet, a trendy restaurant in Fresno's Tower District, two prison parolees, Joseph Davis and Douglas Walker, sped by on a motorcycle and grabbed her purse. Kimber fought. Joseph Davis pulled out a .357-caliber handgun and fired. Kimber died two days after being shot in the ear.

"He pulled out that gun like an insurance man pulls out an insurance card," Mike Reynolds told the *San Jose Mercury News*.

Twenty-four hours after the crime, police surrounded Joseph Davis's home and killed him in a lengthy gun battle. They shot him fifty-two times. Walker was arrested two weeks later. He got a nine-year prison term for being an accessory to murder.

"My daughter had the guts to stand up to those two jerks," Mike Reynolds told the *Los Angeles Times*. "The least I can do is do everything I can to try to prevent this from happening to some other kid."

He hit upon the three-strikes measure,

which he viewed as a way to imprison felons who had made two trips to the lockup only to re-offend. These habitual losers didn't deserve anything more than the odds a baseball player could expect at the plate.

The middle-aged Fresno wedding photographer proposed the idea to his assemblyman. The lawmaker doubted the plan would get passed in committee. Reynolds next loaded friends on four buses and drove to the Capitol in Sacramento to pressure the state leaders. At its first time at bat, the newly born three-strikes concept died in committee just as the lawmaker had predicted. Legislators worried that the measure Reynolds envisioned would lock petty criminals away for life for such minor offenses as burglary and shoplifting.

"They figured they'd listen to me, pat me on the head, say, 'I'm sorry about your daughter,' and send me home," Reynolds told the *Los Angeles Times*.

Reynolds would not go quietly into the night. Next he went to the people and pushed for a state initiative that would leap frog the lawmakers and put the tough crime bill on the election ballot.

"The people who are paid to do this haven't done their job," Reynolds told the *Mercury News*. "It's like going back and re-painting your house after you've already paid someone who did a lousy job."

The idea had support, but lacked the kind of momentum that changes the face of a society, like the state's anti-tax measure, Proposition 13, or the push against drinking and driving fueled by Mothers Against Drunken Drivers (MAAD). A catalyst was needed to make Reynolds's idea take hold. Richard Davis provided the spark. Once Davis's past record became public knowledge, the anti-crime ball was rolling. Soon two-time losers were only a foolish screw up away from a third strike and a potential life sentence. After Polly's body was found, the three-strikes office in Fresno was deluged by so many phone calls that the electronic message system collapsed, according to the *Mercury News*.

Just days after Polly was found, Pete Wilson and Attorney General Dan Lungren made public calls for new laws.

"The only thing that we can do as a memorial for Polly Klaas is to see that she is the last child to suffer this," Wilson said at a press conference. "The only way that you can do that is to really put behind bars for life people who are dangerous."

Wilson had been equally moved by the Reynoldses' tragedy when he visited the grieving family in 1992. He promised Mike Reynolds that he would go after such criminals in a big way. Three strikes paved the way. Not only did it allow Wilson to fulfill his promise to Mike Reynolds, but it gave him and other politicians up for reelection in 1994 a popular platform to get behind. Everyone loves a tough guy, especially when they stand up and take on bullies like Richard Davis, or any other dangerous convict bent on destruction. Three strikes did more than bring a heavy stick down upon the heads of long-time losers.

Michael Huffington, a tall Texas transplant who sought to unseat political mainstay Dianne Feinstein in the 1994 Senate race, added his name and huge pocketbook to the anti-crime cause. He contributed a small fortune to fund the ballot initiative and became co-chairman of Proposition 184, as the three-strikes initiative was officially called.

Huffington was a virtual novice politician. He had moved to California in the early 1990s from his home state of Texas and used a family fortune estimated at $500 million to finance his successful Congressional race in 1992. Though Huffington said he had always been tough on crime, he used three strikes as a springboard to chase a bigger political prize. Who can say if Huffington, or other Sacramento pros seeking office played the anti-crime card because they believed in the law or because it made good newspaper copy? Opinions varied.

The three-strikes idea was suddenly the most popular ride north of Disneyland's

Space Mountain. Talk radio programs across the state beat the drums of war on crime. The state Assembly's Democrat-dominated Public Safety Committee, long known as the killing field for tough crime bills, turned mean.

"We are getting bills out I never thought we'd get out," Republican Assemblyman Richard K. Rainey told the *Los Angeles Times*. "It's definitely a different year."

Facing an election that November, the committee was not about to get soft on criminals as the Assembly prepared for the 1994 session in January. It passed different versions of the three strikes measure along with a bill Rainey proposed making it a felony for convicted sex offenders to avoid registering with police. It also passed a measure toughening the state's pornography laws.

By year's end, the Legislature passed laws that increased prison time for arsonists; required felons to serve at least 85 percent of their terms, not half, as had been the rule; allowed prison managers to confiscate pornographic or hate literature and restricted the ability of inmates to challenge prison regulations; allowed fourteen- and fifteen-year-olds to be tried as adults for serious crimes; and established a 900 telephone number operated by the Department of Justice to allow citizens to learn the communities of residence, physical descriptions, and criminal records of registered sex offenders.

"Right now it's like everyone is just piling on, trying to dream up the most Draconian proposal they can," Democratic Assemblyman Tom Bates told the *Los Angeles Times*. "People need to understand that we have made our sentencing laws in California the toughest in the world and it simply has not worked. It hasn't made us safer."

But Bate's call for calm could not stand up to the fever the Polly Klaas tragedy helped create. Even as the state Legislature drafted various forms of the three-strikes measure—one targeting violent offenders, the other focused on almost any three-time loser—tens of thousands of voters were pledging their support for Mike Reynolds's initiative. No matter what the lawmakers did, Reynolds knew his idea would pass by a vote of the people.

"If people are vengeful and have blood in their eyes, the politicians will reflect that," Bates told the *Los Angeles Times*. "I have to hope the electorate will come off its emotional frenzy and realize that the direction we're going in hasn't worked."

Marc Klaas headed in that direction and initially joined Reynolds on a push for harsh measures, before discovering that the three-strikes initiative would punish nonviolent offenders along with their more dangerous

jailhouse brothers. He later opposed
Reynolds and supported a bill Rainey offered that would be tougher on violent criminals and those convicted of sex offenses and
kidnapping children. The Klaas-Reynolds
tragedy caused hundreds of thousands to
sign the petition for a ballot measure for the
1994 election. Politicians from Sacramento to
Pennsylvania Avenue stood up for three
strikes and waved their support for the idea
at every camera in sight.

Suddenly, a plan that once had no worth
under Sacramento's Capitol dome was the
golden child of 1994. A bill that mirrored
Reynolds's idea was revised and readied for
committee vote. Little did it matter that op-
ponents said low-level crooks would soon
need prison bed space for decades to come,
or that the measure would cost California
billions.

Six months after Wilson penned the bill
into law, more than several thousand cases
had been filed across the state. The net results were just as critics had predicted. Most
of the cases were brought against longtime
felons who now faced long prison terms for
committing petty crimes. Nearly 70 percent
of the new three-strike cases filed deal with
nonviolent crimes like shoplifting or petty
theft.

In Los Angeles, the anti-crime measure ran
amok. Over half the state's three-strike cases

were filed in the sprawling metropolis. The heavy case load clogged the courts and forced delays in civil court matters. More trials were needed since those facing three-strike prosecutions naturally reasoned it was better to take the case to trial than take a plea bargain that had to end with a life sentence.

But the new law held promise as well. RAND, a conservative think tank based in Santa Diana, California, reviewed three strikes and found that it would reduce serious crimes in the Golden State. The think tank's analysis concluded that three strikes could cut crime by as much as 34 percent. The added safety would come with a huge price tag of about $5 billion a year, RAND determined.

The costs did not matter to Reynolds, who said there would be no need to spend money on parks and schools if those places were too dangerous for law-abiding citizens to attend. Human blood was more precious than money.

"You either fill up the prisons or the morgues," he said when asked about the expense connected with three strikes.

No one wanted to sound soft like former presidential candidate Michael Dukakis who once told a national audience that he not only opposed the death penalty, but would keep that opinion even if someone murdered his wife, Kitty. That honesty kept Dukakis in Massachusetts and political obscurity, not the White House.

State legislators lined up behind the measure after polls showed 80 percent of the voters liked the three-strikes idea. In less than a year, Reynolds went from average Joe crime victim to the man of the hour. California House Speaker Willie Brown once snubbed Reynolds and called him a man motivated by crass political gain, according to the *Los Angeles Times*. Yet when the voters favored the Fresno man's grass-roots movement, Brown did an about face and asked Reynolds to appear on his television show. President Clinton invited Reynolds to Washington, ABC's "20/20" television show did a special on his cause. Like Polly Klaas, he made the cover of *People* magazine.

"I wish somebody else would have done this and I would have a daughter," Reynolds told the *Los Angeles Times*. "If I could, even knowing that this law would save a lot of lives, if I could go back and have my daughter back and not have this bill and not have this notoriety and just go back to life the way it was, I'd do it in a heartbeat."

Not everyone loved what Reynolds had to offer. After the Klaas family learned that his measure would provide sentences of up to life in prison for criminals convicted of two serious or violent felonies and a third felony of any type, they turned against it.

"We feel the people of California deserve the choice as to whether or not they want to target serious and violent criminals only, or if they are ready to put people who steal basketballs away for the rest of their lives," Marc Klaas told the media.

"The law stinks," Joe Klaas said of Reynolds's dream child. "Seventy-six percent of all the cases [it affects] are non-violent cases committed by people who have never been violent."

Though devised to protect society from crazed convicts, the law swept up far more petty thieves than would be killers. Minor crimes like petty thefts can and have been prosecuted as third strikes. In Santa Barbara County, one man was prosecuted under the three-strikes law for shoplifting two $60 ties from a department store. After the man broke down on the witness stand, swearing he would beat his addiction to theft, a municipal court judge reduced the petty offense to a misdemeanor and spared the man a possible life term. But another Santa Barbara man still faces a potential life sentence for shoplifting a pair of pliers. Similar stories popped up across that state as prosecutors filed thousands of three-strike cases.

In Van Nuys, California a drug addict infected with the virus that causes AIDS got a life sentence in October 1994 for possessing less than $10 worth of methamphetamine. It was his fourth felony conviction. Even though Superior Court Judge Sandy Kriegler did not want to sentence the thirty-two-year-old man to a life term, under the law he had no choice. The defendant, John Fitzgerald Simmons, had more in common with the average three-strikes candidate than he did with the likes of Richard Davis. True, Simmons had spent most of his adult life in prison, but he had not been violent. His past record included convictions for robbery and residential burglary. He'd only been on the streets for a few days before his drug arrest, according to a report in the *Los Angeles Daily News*. Simmons blamed his troubles on drug addiction.

"I would not want to spend my life dying in prison with HIV that turns into AIDS," Simmons told the *Daily News*. "I would try to do anything I could to straighten my life out and be a better citizen on the streets."

The list of unlikely lifers mounted.

Six months after Wilson signed the anti-crime bill into law, 5,228 three-strike cases had been filed in California, according to the state's District Attorneys Association. Of those, only 24.77 percent were for violent crimes. It took a revolt from state judges to try and slow the tide. Hard-line jurists like retired Air Force Sergeant Barbara Beck, now a municipal court judge in Santa Maria, and Sonoma County Judge Lawrence G. Antolini, who will try the Klaas case, stood against the measure.

Beck called the law "a piece of junk." Antolini said, "It's the duty of the judiciary to interfere if a statute prescribes a penalty out of proportion to an offense."

In August 1994, Antolini declined to imprison Jeffrey Missamore, a twice-convicted felon who faced a third strike for possessing eight grams of marijuana while in the county jail. Instead, the judge issued a 35-page ruling that struck down one of Missamore's priors, citing the defendant's "honest effort to rehabilitate himself." The judge put the convict on probation and referred him to drug rehabilitation. Sonoma County District Attorney, Gene Tunney, who heads the same department that will prosecute Richard Davis, filed an appeal to overturn Antolini's decision.

But the anti-crime movement the Polly Klaas murder helped build did not end with the courts. The cause turned political as the November 1994 election approached. Marc Klaas, like Reynolds, had turned his mourning into a cause. He not only fought for the rights of kidnapped and murdered children, but against those who used human tragedies for political advantage. Three weeks before the election, Marc Klaas told the *San Diego Union-Tribune* that he was "infuriated and frustrated" with politicians, including Pete

Wilson, because they used "Polly's death as a means of making themselves look tough and caring and concerned."

The state's anti-crime wave worked in Wilson's favor. Just a year before his 1994 re-election it appeared the expected Democratic candidate, Kathleen Brown, would trounce Wilson at the polls. Brown's brother, Jerry, once spent two terms in the governor's office. Her father, Pat Brown, had been there too. In 1993, it looked as if the Brown family was about to get its third strike at the top of Sacramento's heap. But Polly Klaas helped change that. Wilson became Mr. Tough-on-Crime. Marc Klaas believes Wilson used his daughter's casket as a steppingstone for political aspirations. Klaas had once been a Wilson supporter. Klaas appeared at the governor's State of the State address in January 1994, at a crime summit with the governor in February and at a crime rally in front of the Capitol in August. By election time, Marc Klaas felt like a pawn.

"She [Polly] was used," Klaas told the *San Diego Union-Tribune*. "I was pulled into this three strikes thing at absolutely the worst possible time, the lowest point of my entire life, at a time when the only thing I could deal with was the fact that she was gone.

"It seems to me politicians only have one bottom line, and that's re-election," Klaas told the *Union-Tribune*. "Everything they do is geared toward getting themselves the kind of money they need and the posturing they need to look good in the eyes of the electorate."

Joe Klaas said he was the first person to find flaws in the Reynolds's three strikes measure. Since then, he has waged war with Wilson and Reynolds. Joe Klaas took on Attorney General Dan Lungren in an effort to get Democrat Tom Umberg to unseat the incumbent. Just weeks before the November election, Joe Klaas appeared in a political ad and virtually accused Lungren of helping murder his daughter for not supporting a plan that would have made it easier for law enforcement officers to track men like Davis.

The voters were in an angry mood on election day.

Three strikes had hit a home run.

The voters didn't care what the liberals said about the tough-on-crime measure. They didn't mind that the courts might soon be clogged with cases. To them, three strikes sounded great. Why worry about jailhouse trash? It was far easier to accept a lock-em-up-and-throw-away-the-key-philosophy than to listen to defense lawyers argue about defendant rights or the cruel and unusual quality of placing a man in prison for life because he stole a slice of pizza. The state didn't want another Polly or Kimber to weep about.

THE LEGAL LEGACY
OF
RICHARD ALLEN DAVIS

FEBRUARY 12, 1973:

Arrested in Redwood City for public drunkenness and resisting a police officer. He was placed on one year summary probation and ordered to pay $25.

APRIL 21, 1973:

Arrested in Redwood City for being a minor in possession of liquor, burglary, and contributing to the delinquency of a minor. Charges dropped and changed to a charge of trespassing. The trespassing charge was later dismissed.

AUGUST 13, 1973:

Arrested by Redwood City Sheriff's deputies when he was found leaning against some hedges in an extremely intoxicated condition. He had apparently urinated in his pants and was extremely dirty. He was transported to county jail and released when he sobered up.

OCTOBER 24, 1973:

Arrested in Redwood City on traffic warrants. While in custody, authorities link Davis to a prior auto theft and burglary. Davis admits to the break-in, saying he was hungry and looking for food. "I knew what I did was wrong," Davis stated, according to court records. "I figured I should get punished for it 'cause I did do it." Davis pleaded guilty to one count of burglary; other charges dropped. He received three years formal probation and six months in county jail.

MAY 13, 1974:

Arrested in South San Francisco for burglary. Sentenced to state prison for a 90-day diagnostic evaluation. Though a prison term is recommended by a county probation officer, the proceedings are suspended while Davis receives alcohol treatment at a Veteran's Administration Hospital. He leaves the treatment program on Sept. 8, 1974.

SEPTEMBER 10, 1974:

Arrested in Redwood City for probation violation involving a felon in possession of a dangerous weapon.

SEPTEMBER 16, 1974:

Davis receives 36 months of probation in

connection with his May 13, 1974 burglary. A one-year jail sentence is suspended.

JANUARY 1975:
Efforts made to get Davis into a Native American alcohol and drug treatment program. The program allows him to leave county jail custody to attend counseling. He fails to return to custody on Jan. 28, 1975 and is charged with probation violation.

APRIL 7, 1975:
Davis admits probation violation and is readmitted to probation under same terms as his Sept. 16, 1974 offense. His probation is extended to five years.

APRIL 11, 1975:
Arrested for probation violation when Davis returns to San Mateo County without prior permission from his probation officer. His probation is revoked and his one-year suspended jail sentence is imposed on August 6, 1975.

JULY 11, 1975:
Davis is arrested for auto theft and possession of marijuana. He receives a 10-day jail sentence.

AUGUST 13, 1975:
Davis's probation is revoked after he is arrested in connection with an Aug. 2 burglary in San Francisco and an Aug. 7 grand theft in San Francisco. He is sentenced to state prison for six years. He receives an indeterminate sentence of six months to fifteen years, but serves only one year at the Vacaville Medical Facility.

SEPTEMBER 24, 1976:
Arrested in Hayward for robbery, kidnapping and attempted oral copulation. While awaiting trial he attempts suicide and is sent on Dec. 8, 1976 to Napa State Hospital. He escapes on Dec. 18.

DECEMBER 20, 1976:
Davis breaks into a Napa home and attacks Marjorie Arlington with a fire poker. Davis breaks into a Napa County animal shelter and steals firearms and animal tranquilizers.
Davis tries to kidnap Hazel Ellis at gunpoint from outside a Napa bar. She pulls a gun and fires at the fleeing Davis.

DECEMBER 21, 1976:
Davis breaks into a La Honda home belonging to Josephine Kreiger. He rummages through Christmas presents, takes

a leather coat, jewelry, and coins worth
$1,000.

DECEMBER 22, 1976:
San Mateo County Sheriff's deputies arrest Davis upon finding him in the brush outside Kreiger's home.

JUNE 1, 1977:
Davis is sentenced to an indeterminate term of one to twenty-five years in state prison for kidnapping Mays.

JUNE 28, 1977:
Davis pleads guilty to receiving stolen property in connection with the Kreiger break-in. He is sentenced to a prison term of six months to ten years.

MAY 5, 1978:
Davis receives sentence of six months to life in connection with the Napa crime spree. All cases stemming from the Mays kidnapping to the Napa felonies run concurrently.

MARCH 4, 1982:
Paroled from the Deuel Vocational Institute in Tracy to San Mateo County.

OCTOBER 12, 1983:
Arrested in Modesto for showing false

identification to a police officer. D.A. declines to prosecute.

JULY 30, 1985:
Sentenced to 16 years in state prison for robbery, kidnapping, and assault of Redwood City woman.

JULY 27, 1993:
Released from the California Men's Colony at San Luis Obispo and paroled to San Mateo County.

OCTOBER 19, 1993:
Arrested in Ukiah for drunken driving.

NOVEMBER 31, 1993:
Arrested near Ukiah for parole violation in connection with drunken driving charges.

DECEMBER 3, 1993:
Pleads guilty to drunken driving charge and receives 30-day jail sentence.

DECEMBER 7, 1993:
Davis is officially charged for the murder of Polly Klaas.

JUNE 19, 1995:
Jury selection is scheduled as Davis's trial begins.